PENNY HODGSON

MIND
FILES

PERCEPTION,
PERSPECTIVE,
& PROBLEMS

Suite 300 - 990 Fort St
Victoria, BC, V8V 3K2
Canada

www.friesenpress.com

ISBN
978-1-5255-2410-3 (Hardcover)
978-1-5255-2411-0 (Paperback)
978-1-5255-2412-7 (eBook)

1. SELF-HELP, PERSONAL GROWTH, SELF-ESTEEM

Distributed to the trade by The Ingram Book Company

INTRODUCTION

You are the author of your life. I'm sure you've heard that before, but do you have a solid understanding of what it means? You have been creating your own life from the moment you took your first breath. If you are living the life you thought you would be – the one you dreamed about – fantastic! However, if you aren't living a life that is 100% fulfilling, and you're ready to learn what you can do to change that – read on.

To change your life, you need to understand why it is that you're not completely satisfied in the first place. Your life is a reflection of what you believe about yourself, others and the world around you. If you believe that you can accomplish great things, you will. If you believe that you can't do anything right, then you won't accomplish very much. If you believe that you are worthy of all that life has to offer, then your life will be abundant, fulfilling, and full of joy. If you believe that people are untrustworthy, cruel, and controlling, then you will attract people who display those properties into your life. If you believe that organizations and governments have power over your life, then you will continue to feel powerless for your whole life. If your thoughts and your true beliefs aren't in perfect alignment, then you are probably unhappy and frustrated more often than not, and you are probably not enjoying life the way you were meant to.

A true belief is just a thought – a perception – that your mind has reminded you of so many times that it plays in the back of your subconscious mind. This is the part of your mind that drives your actions, and this is where the energy that you send out into the universe originates. Your true beliefs are not always the same as what you think you believe (or what you pretend to believe) because they are buried in the depths of your mind. These perspectives were just ideas that you accepted before you were old enough to fully understand them, and these are the things that create blocks in your life.

We are in constant communication with every living thing, every minute of every day. Communication is really just an exchange of energy that is interpreted into meaningful data through our physical senses and processed in our mind at our current level of understanding. The information is then filed in a kind of hard drive, what I refer to as the filing cabinets of our minds, and stored as memories. These memories are then used as a starting point in the mind's process of assessing what is currently going on around us, to us, and inside of us.

As we grow from infants to mature adults, we accumulate information from hundreds of thousands of experiences, form conclusions about each experience, and then condense those conclusions into only a few words or phrases. Inside your mind's storage facility, imagine three filing cabinets: a NEUTRAL cabinet, where every thought or perception is initially filed, a LOVE cabinet, where all the conclusions from your pleasant experiences are filed, and a FEAR cabinet, where all the things that scared you, belittled you, criticized you, shamed you, and otherwise made you feel miserable are filed.

Each time you are exposed to a new thought or experience, your mind looks to previously stored data to use as a reference in helping you understand what you are currently seeing, holding, tasting, hearing, or feeling. If a file exists, it means that you have come across that object, or had a similar experience, prior to the current one. The information in this file is placed in the forefront of your mind, so that the conclusion originally stated in that file is easily retrieved and reinforced. If there is no file, and this is truly a new object or experience, your mind will form a conclusion about the present object or experience and create a new file. Every word we use to describe our experience – which eventually forms our conclusion – is attached to a single dominant feeling. The conclusion and the attached feeling becomes the file our mind then later uses as the reference to interpret current experiences. As far as this mind process is concerned, everything that is not an object is an experience.

Misinterpretations of our current experiences happen easily because our mind is using conclusions from past experiences. The level of understanding at the time of the initial experience is not considered by the mind; the mind simply looks for a reference in the stored data and assumes it is still valid. When the file is retrieved and reinforced, it is then symbolically colored by the reinforced conclusion and feelings. These reinforced conclusions become your true beliefs – your perspectives – and this entire process is how you author your life.

Communication is not limited to language alone. Communication takes many forms, including sight, such as the looks exchanged between two people, or the sight of someone acting, dancing, or singing on a stage. It includes feelings and other sensory information such as smells, sounds, and touch, but the primary mode of deliberate communication between human beings is language.

Words generate feelings, but feelings can also be triggered by a smell, sound or even by witnessing someone else's experience – real or imagined. If the initial experience we had was especially traumatic, the recollection process can bring those intense feelings to the present and create a situation where the person cannot distinguish a past experience from the current one. Additionally, the mind cannot tell if one is reading, hearing, witnessing, tasting, touching, or remembering something; it merely interprets the data and places the appropriate mind file folder in the front of your thoughts. It is then up to you as to whether you accept the data as it's given, or consciously take the time to consider the original source of the data before you react or vocalize your opinion.

The mind's automatic process of not distinguishing old data from newer data is where things can get a little messy: blocks form and problems result. Positive experiences that generate positive feelings are not usually the source of a person's unhappiness or at the root of their personal problems (although they can be). What causes problems in our lives are the negative feelings we carry with us that have been derived from unpleasant past experiences, reinforced through our mind's process, and then form beliefs or rigid perspectives. It is these rigid perspectives that become negatively-colored filters through which we interpret what is happening in the moment. These negative-colored filters heavily influence our personal expectations of current and future experiences, and it is precisely these expectations that are at the root of our problems and conflict.

Recurring failed relationships or marriages are the result of unmet expectations. Going from one miserable job to the next is the result of unmet expectations. Feeling angry, frustrated, and misunderstood all the time is the result of unmet expectations. The things we perceive as problems in our lives are therefore the result of reliving the past, despite our every effort to let the past go.

Life does not have to be difficult, but most people have been conditioned to believe that it is supposed to be that way. We have been told over and over again that life was not meant to be easy, so we not only expect that it won't be or can't be, we accept that it won't be or can't be. We have been told that life is about suffering, so we expect to suffer. We have been told that nothing comes easy, so we expect to have to work hard for everything. We have been told a lot of things that aren't necessarily true, and when we accept these kinds of ideas, we give away our personal power to these ideas that came to our mind from other people. Feeling powerless leads to anger, frustration, resentment, and problems.

PERSONAL POWER

Happiness is only a choice if you believe that you have the power to choose it. If you allow others to think for you, or tell you what you should think, you are giving away the very thing that shapes your life: your personal power.

True peace, contentment, confidence, self-awareness and lasting happiness can't be purchased. You won't find any of those things in a vacation, dream house, fancy car or in that soul mate you think you haven't found yet. Peace, contentment, confidence, self-awareness and happiness are not things. They are all states of being, and when you remember who you really are and reclaim your personal power – you will find peace, contentment, confidence, self-awareness and happiness again.

HEALING IS POSSIBLE

Life can be peaceful, stress free, and enjoyable if we are willing to let go of rigid perspectives. We begin the healing process by learning how and why our thought patterns developed, then we re-evaluate those patterns and determine if we want to keep them or let them go. We can't change things about ourselves if we don't know what needs to change! Try not to be afraid of change; it's just a process of letting go of the old negative patterns, and allowing new and positive patterns to take their place.

Regardless of your religious background or beliefs, a life-changing healing process involves reconnecting with your spirit – the truth of who you are – which in turn allows you to tap into Divine Wisdom and reconnect to God. How you personally define God is completely up to you, but forming a trusting relationship with Him is a crucial step in your healing.

WHO OR WHAT IS GOD?

I've studied a lot of the myths of these cultures around the world, and I can't recall a single negative word in primitive thought with respect to existence or to the universe. World-weariness comes later, with people who are living high on the hog.
~ *Joseph Campbell Pathways to Bliss*

Before you can reconnect with a higher power, you must first have an understanding of what you believe this power to be. You can't completely put your trust in something that you don't fully believe to be safe, protective, and unconditionally accepting.

The theological idea that God made man in his own image is often misunderstood. If you understand God as a being who experiences human feelings like disappointment, jealousy, or anger, and criticizes and judges in the same manner that people do, it will be difficult for you to be willing to put your complete trust and faith in Him. However, if you allow yourself to form your own opinion about what God – the power of creation – might be, then it becomes much easier to be willing to form a relationship with Him.

Rigid perspectives about God can be the result of conditioning. Some folks who have had a strict upbringing in a specific religious doctrine, or who have felt they couldn't live up to God's supposed expectations, may have decided to turn away from Him. Other folks who have found themselves in especially difficult life situations, or have experienced extremely traumatic injuries, illnesses or accidents may also wonder why a loving God would allow these kinds of things to happen, and subsequently abandon any idea of God calling themselves atheists and/or agnostics. When a person's definition and understanding of God includes human characteristics, it is understandable as to why they would choose to blame God for human experiences.

Learning to understand God in a different light, and forming a personal relationship with Him, compels us to let go of the need to blame Him for whatever misfortune we have found ourselves in.

RECONNECTING TO GOD

When your mind is silent and free from anger, worries, and stress, you are able to tap into and receive Divine Guidance from your personal spiritual guide to your spirit. Your spirit is your direct link to all the spirits who have come before and learned through human experience. Every person has their own guardian angel or guide that helps them find their way back to a connection with the collective, or the Holy Spirit if you prefer that name, and then to their higher power – or God, as I refer to it. When your mind is full of chatter, you are not only distracted by that chatter, your subconscious thoughts are controlled by it, and you are not able to sense the connection from your spirit to the Holy Spirit, and to God. You won't be able to hear and feel the guidance from your own spirit, much less tap into the Holy Spirit's wisdom, so you will be relying on and listening only to that part of you that is battered, frightened and lonely. You must make the decision to take conscious control of your thoughts, reconnect first with your own spirit, and then invite the Divine into your life. When you are willing to accept guidance from the Holy Spirit, learn the truth of your painful experiences, and let go of criticism, blame and resentment, the process of healing will begin.

Opinions, ideas, and perceptions change with increased knowledge and understanding. Nothing is absolute! We were intended to be unique creatures, and not duplications of someone else's idea. Every human being has their own set of fingerprints and a specific biochemical makeup that pertains only to them. Although many people share DNA with others, each human being has their own genetic combination that defines them as individuals. The spirit within you is not only directly connected to every other spirit that has lived before and to God, it contains all the knowledge it gained prior to your current life.

THE SPIRITUAL PURPOSE

~Our souls existed apart from the body before they took on human form, and they had intelligence. ~ Socrates

I believe that each person has a purpose that they are meant to fulfill, and that each human form that a spirit embodies has been given challenges to overcome, so that the knowledge they gain in that life can then be shared with all. Each of us learns in our own way, so every spirit's task is equal to all others. As with all education, there are different levels. Younger spirits learn from easier experiences, and older spirits learn from more challenging experiences. Centuries ago, Greek philosopher Socrates posed the idea that our soul – what I refer to as our spirit – recalls knowledge, and in order to recall something, we had to have once known it. This implies that our spirit has lived before and retains the knowledge gained in its previous lives. It also supports the idea that when a spirit takes human form, the challenges that spirit will face will become increasingly more difficult each lifetime. Additionally, it also gives credence to the idea that we are given everything we need to navigate through our current life. These tools come in the form of natural talents.

The further people moved away from a spiritual practice and closer to intellect alone, the more complex life became. The reliance on scientific proof replaced and effectively killed a person's ability to communicate with and trust their spirit, which is usually referred to as one's intuition. The spirit in every person is constantly trying to open a line of communication to the part of the mind that remains unbiased. This type of communication is not easily explained and is often dismissed by the part of the mind that arrives at conclusions. It is a kind of feeling; an instinct that a person has: their intuition, their sixth sense, a gut feeling, or their internal guidance system. It is a sensation that people get when they meet someone they immediately dislike but don't understand why. It is a feeling that can't be intellectually or rationally explained, but one that is always right.

When a person reaches the point in their life where they are sick and tired of being sick and tired, I believe this means that their spirit has finally broken through the protective barriers of the part of the mind that constantly references the FEAR cabinet and is gently guiding them in the direction they need to go to regain their personal power. It is then up to them whether they will choose to follow the guidance of their spirit and reclaim their personal power, or remain in the safety of the familiar misery they are currently living in.

If we truly want to live a life of contentment, joy, and lasting happiness, we must learn to live in the present moment, which means that our mind's process must also *be* in the present moment. We can achieve this by consciously going through the FEAR cabinet in our mind, pulling every file out, reassessing the conclusion contained in it at our current level of understanding, and choosing whether we want to keep it or discard it. Understanding how and why your beliefs came to be what they are is the key in shifting your life from one of unhappy existence to one of unlimited possibilities.

In the pages to follow, you will learn how to discover both positive and negative patterns of behavior that were created through your perceptions of your early experiences, and how these patterns of behavior influence the energy that you now put out into the universe. You'll learn the importance of a conscious and deliberate connection to God, however you choose to define him/her/it and with God's grace, you will be able to experience life from a new perspective

CHAPTER 1

THE HOLY TRINITY

~As I said at the beginning of this tale, I divided each soul into three parts, two of them having the forms of horses and the third that of a charioteer; and one of the horses was good and the other bad, but I have not yet explained the virtue and vice of either…~ Plato

In Phaedrus, Plato explains the soul as having three parts: two horses of opposing nature and a charioteer. The charioteer, he says, is always working to keep the good and evil horses balanced. Being able to balance the good and not so good one experiences is the learning process of life. Think of the mind as being made up of two parts. The first part perceives without judgment; data is collected in an unbiased manner and one is free to experience all that life has to offer. The second part of the mind is the part that forms conclusions and convinces itself that the conclusions it arrived at are truths. This part of the mind is directly connected to the physical body. When the conclusions are negatively-charged perspectives, the body feels the unease and responds by sending out chemicals to help the body deal with that stressor. When this part of the mind is allowed to go unchecked, eventually the body will become exhausted and disease will result.

The spirit lies within the center of the body and is awakened at first breath. This, I believe, is the charioteer that Plato is talking about. The spirit knows that it is directly connected to all living things and responds to the energy surrounding it. The spirit is always doing its best to communicate with and guide its human host by sending out signals in the form of physical sensations. Like God, the spirit never judges, criticizes, or seeks to punish if the mind chooses to go in a different direction; instead, it waits patiently for the mind to balance itself and remember that it is Divinely Guided and protected.

The mind is not an entity of itself – it is one part of the holy trinity that is you – mind, body, and spirit. Learning to reconnect with and follow the guidance of your spirit and reassessing the conclusions your mind formed is how you can reclaim your personal power.

WE BRING MISERY UPON OUR OWN SELF

The true energy that radiates from every living being outwards to every other living being is the energy that draws more of the same experiences to us. This exchange of energy is often referred to as karma or the law of attraction, which is the belief that we get back what we put out into the world. This belief is often misunderstood. Our conscious thought is usually opposite to our true energy, so we end up bringing negative experiences to ourselves rather than the positive ones we intend. This opposition can create a great deal of frustration and unhappiness and can cause people to give up trying to make positive changes in their life.

No one sets out or consciously intends to bring unpleasant situations or experiences to their lives. Everyone wants to be happy, feel safe, and enjoy life, but when we understand our current experiences through a negative filter that we aren't even aware of, positive experiences are temporary at best. We must remove that negative filter altogether in order to change our internal energy and live our life in peace, happiness, and contentment. Once we can fully understand that our true internal energy is created from our perceptions, which become rigid perspectives, and that those rigid perspectives are our true energy, we can consciously take charge of that process, become mindful of every thought, and heal the negative energy that is keeping us from living peaceful and happy lives.

We can only see things through our own eyes, and our eyes see through our past until such time as our past is completely healed. By the time we are adults, we assume we have a solid understanding of everything that happens in our lives, and that we are more than capable of assessing any situation we find ourselves in. What we don't realize, is exactly how our mind processes what is going on around us.

PERCEPTIONS, PERSPECTIVES & PROBLEMS DEFINED

~Miracles rearrange perception and place all levels in true perspective.~
Helen Schucman, A Course in Miracles

Perception, according to the dictionary, is defined as awareness or an understanding of something. Our perception is derived using our senses – sight, smell, hearing, touch and taste, along with our intellectual understanding of that thing or experience at the time of the experience. Our perception, then, is our mind's interpretation of an event, act, or feeling. It is our intellectual conclusion about what we think took place.

Perspective is defined as a view of the relative importance of situations or supposed facts. It is a process of selection or elimination of perceived events or perceived facts – the conclusions we choose to keep and which ones we let go of – along with the weight we assign to them.

Problems arise in our lives when our perception about a person, place, event, or thing becomes a perspective that we are unwilling to let go of.

Our thoughts are our perceptions, and perceptions that have been reinforced multiple times grow into perspectives, and perspectives that have been reinforced multiple times become so rigid that they create problems in our lives.

OPINIONS

An opinion, according to Collins dictionary, is a belief not founded on certainty or proof, but on what seems probable.

Opinions are formed through repetitive thought processes which coincide with repetitive conclusions about similar experiences. Positive emotional reactions come and go with ease, but negative emotional reactions and defensive patterns of behavior are products of deeply-held or rigid opinions that our mind creates after emotionally painful personal experiences. These opinions are then communicated to everyone and everything we encounter, whether we are aware of it or not.

When you have several similar experiences, the mind's process of using the past as a reference causes your thoughts to always arrive at the same conclusion. Your mind retrieved a past similar experience from an already-filed folder and used it as a reference, which then reinforced the original perception creating a perspective. Every time a past experience is reinforced, a symbolic colored filter is added to the original conclusion, and the perspective gains intellectual weight. The original conclusion is justified in your mind every time you appear to be experiencing something similar; your mind tells you, 'This has happened before.'

The memory your mind retrieved and is using could be an experience itself, a feeling, or raw information such as a statistic or definition that you were told or that you read, but the important thing to note here, is that the reference being used was already filed, meaning that perception or understanding took place in the past.

Experiences are always accompanied by emotions, and a person's emotions are the things that determine which colored filter will be added to that file. The colored filter adds symbolic weight, which means the experience is considered by your intellect to be more convincing than definitions or statistics alone. Consequently, experiences will be used more often as references than facts. That is why people will often use the phrase 'it has been my experience' when attempting to justify their stance to themselves or others.

Another important thing to consider about our mind's use of references or memories as a means of assessment is that memories are not necessarily facts. A fact is defined as a provable truth, and proving something is always subject to interpretation.

EMOTIONS

Psychology Professor Paul Ekman, in his book *Emotions Revealed*, explains that there are common characteristics found in emotions, but that each person feels an emotion in their own way. The most important thing, I believe, to understand about emotions is that they are all temporary states of being that change as your perceptions of what you think has happened – or *is* happening – changes. Once you can look back on a hurtful or traumatic experience and understand it from a completely different perspective, you will be able to completely heal that wound and truly move on from it.

Emotions are natural human responses to external stimuli. Although there are times when our minds bury certain emotionally painful experiences until such time we are in a place where we can deal with them, our feelings in general should not be purposely ignored or denied. Feelings are not 'right' or 'wrong' – they simply are what they are at the time. Part of learning to love and honor yourself includes accepting and allowing your emotions to be what they are when they present themselves without allowing yourself to get stuck in a cycle of repetitive misery. When you can allow yourself to cry, be sad, angry, bitter or resentful, you are telling yourself that it is ok to have these feelings, honoring the part of you that feels them. There is a reason you are feeling the way you are, but it might not be as crystal-clear as you think.

Opposing emotions – happy and sad, love and hate, contentment and angst – cannot occupy the same space in your heart or mind at the same time. You can only experience one emotion at a time. No one lives a life without anger, sadness, grief, or bouts of depression, but these feelings are like any other and should pass within a relatively short time frame. When you are holding on to anger, sadness, grief, or depression, there is undoubtedly an underlying cause that you are unaware of or unwilling to deal with.

CHAPTER 2

~ An experience is not even possible without reflection, because 'experience' is a process of assimilation, without which there could be no understanding.
~ Carl Jung, The Autonomy of the Unconscious Mind

THE FILING CABINETS OF YOUR MIND

Imagine again three filing cabinets in your mind. The first cabinet is labelled NEUTRAL. This is where all your random thoughts, raw data, and unbiased information is filed. The second cabinet is labelled LOVE. This cabinet contains files depicting all the experiences that resulted in conclusions that initiated feelings of happiness, joy, and contentment. The third cabinet is labelled FEAR, where all the experiences that resulted in conclusions that initiated feelings of unease, unhappiness, and fright are filed.

Each time you have a new experience, a description of the experience is condensed into a short phrase or sentence, written at the top of the file, and filed in a folder in the NEUTRAL cabinet. The rest of the story is contained in the file, but the mind doesn't use the entire story as a reference, it only uses the condensed phrase, which is the conclusion. Especially emotionally challenging experiences have a greater impact on you, so those will be filed closer to the front of the NEUTRAL cabinet for easier access.

THE PROCESS

The mind's process begins as soon as we have awareness, within a few moments of being born. Initially we learn solely from our five senses – sight, hearing, smell, touch, and taste. Once the ability to think is awakened in our mind, perception of our surroundings begins. Life is simple at the beginning because we have nothing to compare anything to, and we are not yet able to form conclusions. At this stage we are free to experience all that life has to offer, and we enjoy the experience of experiencing!

Then we begin to learn the power of choice. We are utilizing our free will, and we like it. The things that we enjoy we choose more often, and the things we don't like we easily let go of. We assign meaning – or weight – to each and every experience by continuing to choose the things we like over the things we don't like.

> **INITIAL PERCEPTION = I LIKE THIS [object or activity]** ⇨ **FILED IN NEUTRAL CABINET**

> **ONCE CHOSEN AGAIN = I REALLY LIKE THIS [object or activity]** ⇨ **MOVED TO LOVE CABINET**

> **ONCE CHOSEN AGAIN = I TOTALLY LOVE THIS!! [object or activity]** ⇨ **COLORED FILTER ADDED TO THE PERCEPTION – SYMBOLICALLY GIVING GRAVITY OR WEIGHT TO THE ACTIVITY**

Imagine a baby in a crib surrounded by toys. As the infant picks up each toy, their mind is assessing the experience of touching, tasting, and moving the toy about. The toy that generates the strongest positive emotion will be the toy that the baby chooses more often. Sounds simple right? At this point there is no complicated process. It's an easy choice; the baby likes the toy, so they play with it more often!

The initial perception is: 'I like the sound this toy makes when I shake it.' The conclusion becomes TOY = FUN, and it is filed in the NEUTRAL cabinet.

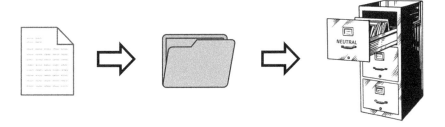

The second time the child picks up that toy, the mind's interpretation of the experience might be something like: 'I see this toy and, I remember playing with it.'

At the sight of the toy, the baby's mind had already pulled the folder with the conclusion: TOY = FUN and placed that in the forefront of the mind. The mind is then reminded of the story in the file that describes the enjoyment at shaking the toy. The baby picks up the toy, shakes it again and the sound causes the baby to laugh, which stirs up a fun feeling. The recollection process, combined with the similar feelings reinforces the original conclusion that the toy is indeed fun, and the entire file is now moved into the LOVE cabinet.

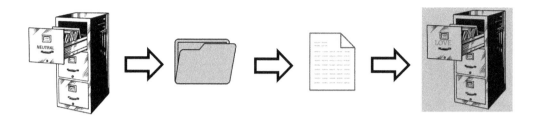

The third similar experience becomes: I chose to play with this toy because I now know that I like the sound it makes when I shake it. The conclusion that the toy is fun to play with was once again retrieved from the LOVE cabinet at the sight of the toy. The conclusion is again reinforced by the repeat experience of playing with it and enjoying it. A colored filter symbolizing the intensity of the enjoyment is added to the file, and the file is once again stored in the LOVE cabinet for future reference.

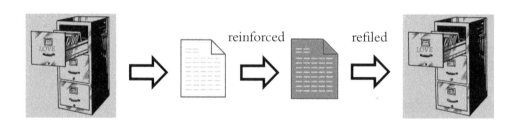

reinforced   refiled

ASSESSMENTS & DATA COLLECTION

The mind's process can only assess experiences at a person's current level of understanding. Feelings are added to this assessment when a person reaches the age where they can decide which feeling feels appropriate. It is the feeling that gives weight to the overall assessment or conclusion of the experience.

Certain feelings will get attached to a certain word or a group of words, and the combination of those words along with the feelings can end up carrying a great deal of weight. For example, suppose as a young child your mother hugs you every time she tells you she loves you. Her words and her physical action feel comforting and pleasant. The first time it happened, the description of feeling good after being held by your mother would have been filed in the NEUTRAL cabinet. The next time your mother picked you up, told you she loved you, and you again experienced the pleasant feelings, the file containing the conclusion of feeling good when your mother held you will be retrieved from the NEUTRAL cabinet, reinforced and validated, and then moved over to the LOVE cabinet.

The third time your mother picked you up and told you she loved you, the file would have been retrieved from the LOVE cabinet, reinforced, and validated once again, and to symbolize the intensity of the feeling, a colored filter is added to the file. With each additional similar experience, more colored filters are added to the folder and a rigid perspective – an expectation – is born.

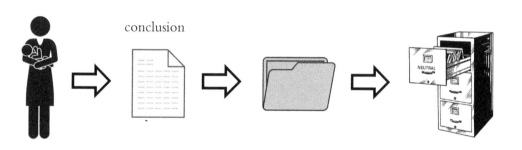

conclusion

The CONCLUSION/DESCRIPTION is: My mom picked me up and held me close to her body. It felt good to be held by her.

The description is then filed in the NEUTRAL cabinet

 The file containing the description of being held is brought to the forefront of thought. The image is now in your mind

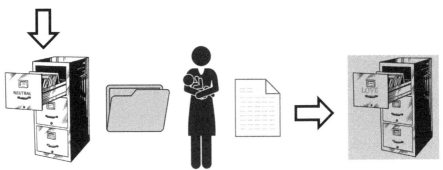

Mom picks me up and holds me close to her ⇨ my mind looks in the NEUTRAL cabinet for a previous similar event ⇨ retrieves the conclusion: My mom picked me up and held me close to her body. It felt good to be held by her. ⇨ Reinforced conclusion: It feels good to be held ⇨ file moved to LOVE cabinet

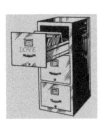

Mom picks me up ⇨ my mind recalls feeling good when I am picked up and held ⇨ looks in LOVE cabinet, retrieves the file ⇨ reinforces the previous conclusions: It feels good to be held ⇨ adds a colored filter to the file and files it back in the LOVE cabinet

As far as our mind's process is concerned, everything that is not an object is an experience. Experiences either nurture us (thereby ending up in our LOVE cabinet) or create a feeling of unease in us (ending up in our FEAR cabinet). We either feel good or we feel bad, but we cannot feel both good and bad at the same time. Every conclusion we arrive at is filed in folders labeled with the word or phrase that best describes the experience from our personal vantage point.

Feelings or emotions are much more powerful than words alone, so they contribute heavily to our interpretation or perception. We also learn by watching what other people are experiencing and interpreting what we think they are feeling by examining their body language and listening to what they are saying. We must remember, though, that our mind is always interpreting what is happening using the folders we have created in our own minds.

CHAPTER 3

~We see things not as they are, but as we are. ~ Author unknown

REFERENCES CAN ONLY COME FROM OUR OWN CABINETS

Our mind assesses what we think the words and actions of another towards us means by intellectually interpreting what we are seeing in the person's facial expressions and overall body language, including the tone of their voice, and their word choice. These are all key indicators as to which folders our mind will retrieve and from which cabinet the file is retrieved from. Our mind also assesses other people's experiences, even when those experiences have nothing to do with us.

For example, let's say we are witnessing a quarrel between our friend and their partner, and we find our own emotions triggered by our friend's experience. Our mind can only access folders from the filing cabinets of our own mind to use as references, so if we are negatively emotionally affected by what we are witnessing, there is a past experience that appears to be similar to our friend's experience filed in our FEAR cabinet. That past experience is really what is causing our emotions to be triggered – not the situation in front of us.

We are always seeing what is going on around us through our own filters. Our mind finds what it thinks is a similar experience and brings that folder to the forefront of our consciousness. We think we are being empathetic towards our friend, when in reality, we are reliving our own experience through theirs. We tell ourselves that we have bonded closer

with our friend and find comfort in believing we are not alone in the feelings of that shared experience. The thing is, we have made an assumption
of what we think the other people involved must be thinking based on
the sensory data our mind interpreted and assessed, before our friend even
begins to tell their story to us about their argument.

The thing to really try to grasp here, is that we are always experiencing
through our own filters, because our mind can only access our personal
file folders. If our emotions are triggered by what we think someone else
is experiencing, it means that there is a file in either the LOVE cabinet, or
the FEAR cabinet that needs to be consciously pulled out and reassessed.

REPEATED EXPERIENCES ARE NOT ALWAYS WHAT WE EXPECT

Remember the folder you created when your mother hugged you and told
you she loved you? The expectation of pleasant feelings was established with
the repetitive action of being held close to another body. Let's suppose that
experience happened so often in your early life, that the conclusion written
in your mind's folder was condensed into two short words: HOLDING =
LOVE. When someone puts their arms around you and holds you, your
mind retrieves the folder, places it in the forefront of your mind where it
instantly concludes the current experience should be pleasant and loving.

Now, if someone holds you and your body feels pain, the resulting
emotion would not be pleasant. Your mind would initially be confused,
then curious as to what is happening. The new conclusion might be something like: so-and-so picked me up and held me, but they held me so tight
they hurt my arms and I was afraid.

This experience would be filed in the NEUTRAL cabinet because the
experience of being held combined with unpleasant feelings has not yet
occurred. The next time you were held by someone where you again felt
uncomfortable and afraid, your mind may now arrive at the conclusion
that the person *intended* to hurt you, and the word 'hold' might be changed
to 'grabbed' to differentiate the good feeling experience from the bad.
Additional information such as the words the person used as they were
holding you, the tone of their voice, and the look on their face will be kind

of highlighted or emphasized in some manner in the file, so that your mind can use this information as a warning the next time someone attempts to pick you up or hold you. This folder might now be entitled 'GRABBED = SCARY', and would then be placed in the FEAR cabinet.

The acts of being held with their opposing conclusions are now described in both cabinets. If the experience of being grabbed happened again, and the same or similar uncomfortable feelings accompany the experience, a yellow caution filter or other color that fits your uneasy feeling will be added to that folder to further symbolize danger or something that should be avoided. If you have a third experience, another colored filter will be added to the folder, and a perspective that being grabbed should be avoided at all costs will form.

1st time = I was picked up and held but instead of it feeling good, it hurt my arms and I was scared ⇨ filed in NEUTRAL cabinet

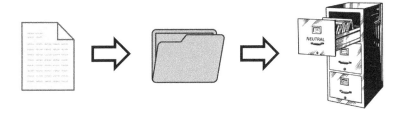

2nd time = So-and-so grabbed me and I couldn't get away because they were holding my arms too tight, and it hurt me, and I got scared. He/she must have meant to hurt me because he/she sure looked mad and sounded angry. The resulting conclusion becomes: I FEEL SCARED WHEN so-and-so grabs a hold of me because they want to hurt me. The file is moved from the NEUTRAL cabinet to the FEAR cabinet.

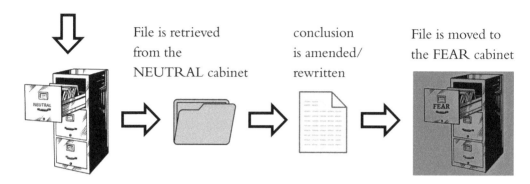

File is retrieved from the NEUTRAL cabinet

conclusion is amended/ rewritten

File is moved to the FEAR cabinet

3rd time = As so-and-so approaches, the file labelled I FEEL SCARED OF so-and-so is pulled from FEAR cabinet, the conclusion is reinforced and a colored filter added to symbolize the intensity of the fear. The file is re-filed in the FEAR cabinet.

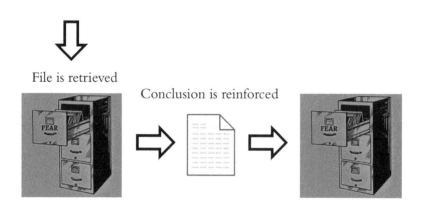

File is retrieved

Conclusion is reinforced

IT'S NOT ALL BAD STUFF

Accomplishments, favorite things, and enjoyable activities also have folders and collect colored filters symbolizing the intensity of the pleasure you felt after the experience. These folders are filed in the LOVE cabinet.

Imagine a folder labelled PLAYING WITH -------- MAKES ME HAPPY. Inside the file is a description of all the people and toys you played with that made you feel happy. Your personal definition of the words play and happy will be well established by the time you are three or four years old. In the first few years of life it is easy to arrive at happy because every experience is new, and you are in the beginning stage of collecting data. When you are able to assign a name and then a feeling to the activities which are more enjoyable than others, the colored filters will also start accumulating in each file. Once you are an adult, the word 'play' will take on a different meaning for you, and might include activities such as sports, sex, gambling, shopping, drinking alcohol, or taking recreational drugs.

When you are not feeling happy and make a conscious decision to change your current feeling state, your mind will look to the folder labelled PLAYING WITH ----------MAKES ME HAPPY to find experiences that will change your feeling from sad to happy. Each time you choose an experience from the PLAYING WITH -----------MAKES ME HAPPY and succeed in changing your sadness to happiness, that file is moved closer to the front of the drawer and given a colored filter, which reinforces and validates the experience. A positive perspective and an expectation has now formed.

Other folders in your LOVE cabinet will contain conclusions that describe how you feel about yourself when you've accomplished some-thing that you've worked hard at. If you are praised for your achievements, you may put that conclusion in a folder labeled I FEEL LOVED WHEN- --------- and/or I CAN DO ----------. Your LOVE cabinet folders will continue to gather a lot of files when you are very small, but at some point, people will say things to you that create doubt in your mind about being loved or what you can do. If you have a healthy support system the doubt may easily be dismissed, but if you do not have a healthy support system, the doubt will grow.

By the time you are ten years old, the number of folders filed in all three cabinets could be in the hundreds of thousands depending on how many people, places and things you have encountered by that time. The exact way your mind sorted the files between the cabinets will depend on your personal understanding of each experience and the resulting conclusion.

Tidbits of information that you've gathered along the way are also stored in the filing cabinets of your mind. Information from subjects that piqued your interest in school, or subjects you deemed valuable enough to study on your own, will get stored in a file for future and cross-reference. These filed are kept in the NEUTRAL cabinet and might be under the heading of THINGS THAT COULD HELP ME ARE -----------. Neutral information provides you with the tools you need to complete tasks. Once you are old enough to join the workforce, relative information contained in these files will be retrieved and reinforced. The files themselves may stay in the NEUTRAL cabinet unless or until you assign a feeling to the tasks you are performing. If you determine that you love your job, then all files relating to your job experience will end up in your LOVE cabinet. If you don't enjoy your job, feel undervalued, overworked and underpaid, then the files will end up in the FEAR cabinet.

INTENSE FEELINGS DISTORT CONCLUSIONS

If an experience is especially frightening, the file could become rigid right from the start due to the intensity of the emotion you felt at the time. Frightening experiences create a need for immediate safety, which causes your mind to try to come up with techniques that will avoid similarly scary situations in the future.

Our understanding of excessively emotionally painful or frightening experiences is always distorted, because our mind's process looked for a file from the past which would have warned us and didn't find one. There was nothing to reinforce or validate either, but our mind instantly knew it didn't want to have a similar experience again. If a current experience appears to be similar enough to the past experience that you feel fear rising in your being, your mind won't intellectually assess your current experi-ence. Instead it will reinforce the previous conclusion, even if the previous conclusion was formed many years prior when your level of understanding was considerably less.

Emotional intensity combined with the conclusion formed determines whether the current experience warrants a new folder of its own, or is similar enough to be added to a past one. Folders that hold multiple similar experiences that caused you to feel the same intense emotions will be ref-erenced more often, because the emotions were the same. When previous experiences are validated by similar emotions through this process of rein-forcement, the original perception gains strength.

BEHAVIOR PATTERNS DEVELOP

As your intellect matures and you develop reasoning skills, your mind will devote an entire drawer to behaviors that help you avoid unpleasant feelings. This drawer might be labelled 'DEFENSES THAT WORK' or 'WHEN THINGS GO WRONG.' Inside this drawer are folders containing descriptions of actions that you took that helped you avert punishment and/or avoid unpleasant feelings. There may also be folders containing experiences that describe painful experience – such as touching something hot and being burned, illnesses, accidents, or surgeries – as well as purely emotion-ally difficult experiences like being ridiculed, judged, or criticized. It is our nature to do our best to avoid pain (physical or emotional) and to survive. The desire for survival is an instinct shared by all living creatures, but what makes humans different from every other living being, is our ability to think, deduce, and reason.

CHAPTER 4

THE FAMILY CONNECTION

~ The Lord, the Lord, a God merciful and gracious, slow to anger,
and abounding in steadfast love and faithfulness, keeping steadfast love
for the thousandth generation, forgiving iniquity and transgression
and sin, yet by no means clearing the guilty, but visiting the iniquity
of the parents upon the children, and the children's children, to the third
and the fourth generation. ~ The Bible – Exodus 34

There is a common belief that self-defeating behavior patterns, as well as physiological disease, runs in families. For example, children who grow up in abusive homes are said to be more likely to become abusers themselves. Children who grow up in homes with an addict have a higher probability of becoming an addict themselves. This happens because the files in the FEAR cabinet of both parent and children contain experiences that arrived at self defeating conclusions before an age where those self-defeating conclusions could be challenged. The environment introduced the idea, and the mind's process reinforced the idea multiple times until it was a rigid perspective.

There is also a common acceptance that disease passes down through genes, and for the people who accept that idea without question, there will also be an acceptance of the disease.

We are beings made up of mind – our thoughts, body – the living structure that carries us around, and spirit – the essence of who we are. Each part affects the other. Disease in our bodies is the consequence of the effects of our conclusions on our bodies. If we believe that we are destined to become an addict, an abuser, or to develop cancer because one of our parents is or did, the power of that belief will make that conclusion come true for us.

As a child, you relied on the people who were in charge of your well being to supply your every need. When you wanted to be held, fed, or changed, you cried and your caregiver had to determine what to do based on their level of understanding of what your basic needs were. They could only do what they knew how to do based on the files in their filing cabinets. If the people who cared for them were not nurturing, then they would neither know how to be nurturing nor understand the importance of it. If the people who care for you were treated with abuse, then despite their best efforts to not do what was done to them, there will be some level of abuse – verbal, emotional or physical – because those are the files that their minds use as references.

The conclusions you arrived at in response to how you were raised will determine how you choose to raise your own children, and how you respond to other people's children. Let's say your parents were overly strict. Eventually, when you reached the age where you wanted to exert your own independence, you probably arrived at a conclusion that described how 'controlling' your parents were. The more you reinforced the conclusion that your parents were controlling, the bigger the desire to gain control of your own life became. You may have made a decision to be much more lenient with your own children. If you chose to raise your children completely opposite to how you were raised and allowed them to do whatever they wanted, you might wonder years later why your children have no respect for you or your authority. If you see other people's children misbehaving and running wild in a department store, you might think to yourself, 'Gee, why doesn't that parent control their kids?' Your beliefs about children were in response to the conclusions you arrived at about your own childhood, just as your parents' beliefs were in response to their conclusions about their own childhood.

LEARNING BEGINS IN INFANCY

As an infant, every day you gradually became aware of your surroundings. You explored everything around you by hearing, sight, and touch. As you explored, you made simple decisions about whether you liked certain things or didn't like them by the way you felt when you encountered them, both emotionally and physically. The things you didn't like you would simply leave alone, and the things you did like you would interact with more often, such as a favorite rattle, stuffed toy or blanket. Life and decision making started out being a very simple exercise.

As you grew and discovered you have a mind that can think and reason, things became far more complicated. The more you learned, the more facts you gathered, and the more intellectual you became, the more convoluted your conclusions were at the end of each experience. Your ability to accept things the way they are becomes increasingly distorted and impaired, because the mind's process is one of comparing, judging, and criticizing things against already-developed perspectives.

WORDS, IMAGES AND ACTIONS

We learn words initially by associating the word with an object or activity. The first folders that were created in our minds were very simple. They contained an image of an object and a single word to describe it. The folders start out as basic needs, although as an infant you aren't consciously aware of what a basic need is. Your instinct tells you that you are without something that your physical body requires. You simply feel thirsty, don't feel well, etc. The only method of communication you have as an infant is to cry. When you start crying, the person in charge of your well being has to determine what your need is. If they think you are thirsty, they might hold up a bottle where you can see it and say: drink? The image of the bottle tells you that that thing will satisfy your thirst. The image of the bottle will go in the folder marked I NEED ----------TO FEEL BETTER, in this case, a drink. It's not the liquid inside the bottle – the water or milk – it's the image of the bottle that your mind uses as a reference. You are given a bottle, you suck on the nipple, fluid flows out of the bottle and into your mouth. Your thirst is satisfied, and you are content. At some point, when you can differentiate between types of liquid, the name of the liquid you enjoy the most will replace the basic image of the bottle. The entire conclusion will be moved from the NEUTRAL cabinet to the LOVE cabinet and placed in a folder labeled: I LIKE ----------. As you taste new and different liquids, and form new likes and dislikes, those conclusions will be added to the I LIKE ----------folder, or I DON'T LIKE ---------- folder.

As we grow, the images and the words associated with them become our vocabulary. The more attention you received from your parents, siblings, and other caregivers, and the more experiences you had, the more images and words get filed in the filing cabinets of your mind. Remember, all folders are initially filed in your NEUTRAL cabinet because the folders contain only raw data. It is when that data is once again brought to the forefront of your mind through the retrieval process and a similar conclusion drawn, that it becomes something more than data.

Let's go back to the I NEED ----------TO FEEL BETTER folder. The very first time your body became uncomfortable, you believed you were without something that you needed to feel better. You cried, someone gave you the very thing you needed, and you immediately felt better. Although you are not aware or conscious of the process, this folder is being accessed each time your mind determines you need something. What you have learned from this process is:

⇨ I make the sound of crying = attention = I feel better.

The conclusion was you gained whatever it was you felt you needed by crying, and you have now reinforced a means of communication.

Depending on the type of home life you had, you may not have had a lot of other interaction with a caregiver unless you were crying. Remember, your caregivers did what they knew how to do based on their own experiences. If they were aware of the importance of personal interaction, they would have interacted with you as much as possible, but if they didn't realize the importance of interaction, or felt their needs were more important than yours, you wouldn't have accumulated many folders in your mind's cabinets until you were placed in an environment that was more personally stimulating.

LEARNING ABOUT CONSEQUENCES

We learn about consequences from our caregivers, peers, and other people we consider to be authority figures in our lives. When we touch or say something we shouldn't as an infant, an authority figure disciplines us by using forceful or aggressive language in a louder tone of voice than they would normally speak to us in. Perhaps the person said NO! while performing an action such as slapping our hand or shaking a finger in our direction. Because the word NO! is spoken louder and with a sharpness in tone that is intended to be alarming, you immediately understand you shouldn't be doing or saying that thing. If your hand was slapped at the same time as the person said the word 'NO!' the slap would have startled you and you would have felt physical pain. The intensity of the slap and the volume of the person's voice as they said the word NO! would have stirred up one or more feelings inside you, and the combination of tone of voice and physical pain would have had more emotional intensity and made much more of a lasting impression on you. When you were very young and didn't yet know that you determined the intensity of your own feelings, the startled feeling would have happened then quickly dissipated. The initial conclusion you arrived at would have been filed in the NEUTRAL cabinet in a folder labeled DO NOT DO ----------. The next time this kind of scenario happened, the folder labeled with the phrase DO NOT DO would have been pulled from the NEUTRAL cabinet and moved to the FEAR cabinet.

Feelings such as fear, guilt, and shame are common emotional reactions when someone you view as an authority punishes you for doing something they think you shouldn't be doing. The feeling of guilt or shame that you experience in some cases is sometimes dictated to you by the person that is punishing you. That person might have said something like, 'You should be ashamed of yourself,' so the awful feeling you are experiencing becomes shame in your mind. The statement 'you should be' teaches you to feel guilt or shame, so when you are chastised or punished after doing or saying something you shouldn't have, and experienced fairly intense feelings, a symbolic colored filter is immediately added to the I SHOULD BE ASHAMED OF MYSELF BECAUSE---------- folder, an original conclusion reinforced, and a perspective formed.

By now, I hope it is becoming clearer to you how your understanding of every event or experience you have had is put in a kind of folder in your mind, labelled with a word or phrase that makes sense to *you* that describes the event or experience.

CHAPTER 5

~We speak of 'knowing' something when we succeed in linking a new perception to an already existing context…~ Carl Jung

It's important to understand that every experience you are about to have is being referenced against a supposedly-similar previous one. Remember, the mind uses comparison as a thought process to help you understand what is happening in your current space and time. Every time an initial perception is reinforced, the power of that initial conclusion gains strength. The folders that contain the strongest emotional conclusions are filed in the front of the cabinets for easy and fast retrieval and referenced more often as a result.

The past appears to repeat itself because the mind is using the past as a reference as it is assessing what your eyes are seeing, your ears are hearing, your skin is touching, and your mouth is tasting. At the exact instant your mind receives the information from your eyes and ears, it has already pulled a file that appears to contain a similar description and put that file in the forefront of your mind. The mind reminds you of what was in that file, so an expectation is already forming.

DEVELOPING AVERSION TECHNIQUES

Everyone learns by testing out ideas. If other people easily accept your idea, the conclusion about that idea will be positive and the resulting conclusion will be filed in the LOVE cabinet. If an idea is rejected, the resulting conclusion will end up somewhere in your FEAR cabinet. Rejection of an idea is different than personal rejection, but most people experience what it feels like to have an idea rejected before they are old enough to understand the difference.

Let's say you are playing in your bedroom with your younger sister. You draw a huge flower on the wall with a crayon while your sister is playing across the room with dolls. At some point, you join your sister playing with the dolls. Your father walks in the room and asks both of you who drew the huge flower on the wall. You can hear that he is not happy by the tone of his voice, and you can see by the look on his face that the beautiful drawing of the flower on the wall made him angry.

Your mind, in an instant, has already searched your FEAR cabinet, retrieved a folder labeled I FEEL AFRAID WHEN----------, and found a file containing a description of a time before when your dad was angry with you and you were punished. Your mind reminds you that there was a similar look on your dad's face, a similar tone in his voice when he spoke, and the type of punishment you received. The intensity of the emotion you felt as a result of being punished before will determine what you choose to do to avoid punishment this time.

It is a natural instinct to do what you can to avoid feeling unpleasant feelings. No one likes the feeling of being in trouble. Hearing a parent say "I'm really disappointed in you" when they've caught you doing something they disapprove of never feels good, so the desire to avoid that feeling causes us to develop aversion techniques.

Let's suppose that to avoid getting in trouble, you tell your dad that your sister drew the flower on the wall. Your dad asks you if you are telling the truth about who drew the picture and you insist you are. Your dad explains to you that your sister couldn't have drawn a flower like that, tells you that you shouldn't lie, that only bad people lie, and spanks you. The spanking hurts your feelings and your bum; you experienced physical pain, embarrassment, disappointment, and you cried because you were caught telling a lie and punished.

The aversion technique failed, and the resulting conclusion is: 'To avoid getting in trouble, I need to come up with a better story.'

A description of the experience might say something like: 'When I think I'm going to get in trouble and I make up a story to avoid trouble, I get a spanking and a spanking is painful. I felt guilty for lying, disappointed that my drawing wasn't appreciated, and shame and embarrassment from having my bum spanked in front of my little sister.'

CONCLUSION = WHEN I MAKE UP STORIES TO AVOID GETTING IN TROUBLE = PHYSICAL PAIN + DISAPPOINTMENT + SHAME + GUILT = I'M BAD

The next time you try to avoid getting into trouble for something and lie, get caught, and receive the same kind of punishment – the original conclusion that was filed in the folder labelled WHEN I MAKE UP STORIES TO AVOID GETTING INTO TROUBLE---------- is reinforced, which also reinforces the emotions of guilt, shame and embarrassment increasing their power. The conclusion of 'I'm bad' is also reinforced, and the line between *your action* and *you* becomes blurry. If you keep testing the strategy of telling tall tales or lying to avoid getting into trouble, and always get found out and receive some form of punishment, eventually the act of lying will be filed in a drawer marked: DO NOT DO---------- and filed in the FEAR cabinet. The intensity you assigned to your feelings of disappointment, shame and guilt will determine whether you conclude that lying is something you want to try again.

Rejection of an idea doesn't necessarily have to end in physical punishment for the file to end up in the FEAR cabinet and be something you want to avoid in the future. Being told to stand in the corner, locked in closet, publicly humiliated, or yelled at can have the same emotionally devastating effect, regardless of a person's age.

When we have experienced something that hurts us either physically, emotionally or a combination of both, our mind attempts to protect us from experiencing the same kind of emotional pain by testing defense mechanisms. Once one or more defensive mechanisms prove their worth and become perspectives, these defensive perspectives become patterns of behavior used as protective measures. These protective measures are our body guards who might have helped us escape similar hurtful experiences when we were not able to defend ourselves for one reason or another, but they can also intervene when they are no longer needed.

FEELINGS ARE FEELINGS

It's important to note that all emotions can be equal in their intensity. Happy or joyful feelings are just as intense as sadness or fear, so it's not necessarily that negative feelings are referenced more often (although it usually seems to most people that this is the case).

Every person creates files and stores them in the cabinet that makes sense to them. A file labelled I FEEL HAPPY WHEN---------- could exist in both the FEAR cabinet and the LOVE cabinet. Things that allow a person to feel happy and content would obviously be filed in the LOVE cabinet, but if the feeling itself was elusive, or if happy events turned into frightening events because a family member became angry and/or abusive, there would also be a file in the FEAR cabinet.

LABELS

When a conclusion appears to satisfy an uncomfortable feeling, that conclusion is reinforced in the mind's process every time the mind thinks it is experiencing something similar. When the thought process involves people, there is usually an accompanying label in the resolution – He/she is a ----------. When labels are used in conjunction with people problems result.

Smart, stupid, skinny, fat, clumsy, good, bad, abused, addict, anorexic, antisocial, bully, codependent, control freak, depressed, extrovert, introvert, gay, straight, asexual, bisexual, racist, xenophobic, psychotic, obese, and stressed out! These are just a few of the labels that make their way into the mind's conclusions. Labels are used all the time by everyone, and the use of labels has become so important in our society today, that an entire generation of people have become lost in them.

The process of assigning labels to people originated in the medical community. Labels were, and still are created so medical professionals can identify which set of symptoms belong to a patient. When labels left the medical community and found their way into mainstream vocabulary, they became a means of personal identification, and labels used in this manner are problematic.

People willingly label themselves and others hoping it explains or justifies certain personality traits and behaviors. Some people are eager to display their label for others to see, hoping that they will either be immediately accepted, or be given special privileges. What often happens is the opposite. They are ostracised and segregated so they become frustrated, hurt and angry. Some people think that once they publicly state their label, such as one that describes a behavior pattern, they are then relieved from having to do anything about their label.

Labels divide people into categories and categories are more about differences than similarities; exclusion rather than inclusion. Whether people are put into categories or assigned one makes no difference. Categories provide an opportunity for people to decide what they like and don't like. With selection comes judgment which, where people are concerned, creates problems.

CONSEQUENCES OF LABELS

Everyone wants to believe they matter in this world – who they are, where their place is in society – and to be recognized for the thing or things that make them unique. Self worth and self love have become one and the same in the minds of most people, but they have completely different meanings. Self worth is your personal understanding of belonging and knowing that you have a purpose in this world, and self love is a description of all of the things you do to nurture and take care of yourself, like eating properly, getting plenty of exercise and paying attention to your spiritual needs.

People who have been labeled – by themselves or others – struggle a bit more with self love and self worth than those who haven't. Certain labels carry with them an image or popular perception of that label that might not be entirely accurate. For example, some people might picture an addict as a homeless person that chose alcohol or drugs over a normal life, or a depressed person as one who cries all the time. Labels such as these can hold a negative connotation in some people's minds, despite efforts to change the general perception of these kinds of labels. Labels that are intended to divide, such as cultural, racial, and gender labels cause problems when a person identifies so strongly with that label that they cannot see themselves apart from it.

CHAPTER 6

~ Consciousness of pleasure has grown up with all of us from our infancy, and therefore our life is so deeply imbued with this feeling that it is hard to remove all trace of it. ~ Aristotle, The Nicomachean Ethics

EXAMINING EXPECTATIONS

Expectations are at the root of all unhappiness, and the drive to be in a constant state of happiness is the consequence of a skewed perception, and an unbalanced life experience. It simply means that the mind is referencing files in the FEAR cabinet far more often than the files in the LOVE cabinet. The idea that one needs something other than what they have in order to be happy is the root of expectation.

Occasions are the best example of an experience that creates expectations, because occasions almost always carry with them a variety of feelings, images, tastes, smells, and sounds. It is the combination of these feelings, images, tastes, smells, and sounds that create a more memorable experience, so the files usually have colored filters from the get go. Some occasions might have all positive or good feelings, as in a wedding or other kind of celebratory party, while others contain mostly sad or negative feelings, as in a funeral. Other occasions may have a mixture of both.

One example of an occasion that everyone can relate to, and that has a variety of intense emotions is your birthday. Inside the folder labeled IT'S MY BIRTHDAY! are descriptions of every birthday experience you've had so far, along with all the feelings you experienced. If you had a party every year on your birthday and continued to have parties well into your early adulthood, the conclusions in your files probably include a description of fun and games, balloons, presents, cake, and ice cream – all the objects that were included in the experience, along with each and every feeling you felt at the time.

An expectation that there will be a party every year on your birthday would have been established by your third consecutive party as the result of multiple occurrences, and the colored filter that you filed along with your conclusions will be a color that describes fun, joy and happiness. If and/or when the parties stopped happening on your birthday, the feeling of being let down, along with all the words that you use to describe the disappointment you felt, will be added to that folder, and a new folder will be created and filed in the NEUTRAL cabinet. If you experience another disappointing birthday, the file will be moved from the NEUTRAL cabinet to the FEAR cabinet, and a colored filter representing your disappointment will be added. If the disappointing experience continues for several years in a row on your birthday, or if the feeling of being let down holds more power for you than the joy of initial event, the folder initially filed in your LOVE cabinet will not be referenced again. Instead, the folder now filed in your FEAR cabinet becomes the dominating file for reference. The initial conclusion in that folder could be more of a question than a statement. It might say something like 'What did I do wrong?', or 'I must have been really bad'.

In trying to understand why a party was not arranged for your birthday, your mind would have run several different scenarios as to why you were forgotten you on your special day. Depending on your developing dominating personality type, which is determined by the conclusions you arrived at and filed away, the initial conclusion as to why the party was missed would have either been one of self blame – I must have been bad because I didn't get a party – or blame would have been assigned to someone else – so and so is bad because he/she didn't arrange a party for me .

The victim personality type blames others for unmet expectations, and they also believe that they were powerless to fulfill that need for themselves. The majority of files in their cabinets form conclusions that started out saying 'I must not be good enough because---------', and end up becoming 'it's ----------'s fault that I can't do/have ----------. The opposing personality type is much more defiant, so the conclusions in their files say 'screw them! I don't need their stupid party anyway.' These kinds of conclusions result in a warrior personality. Both personality types have the same underlying cause – unmet expectations – they just express them in an opposing manner.

As young children, there isn't yet the intellectual reasoning capacity to understand that there might be extenuating circumstances that prevent their expectation from being fulfilled. The intensity of the feeling of disappointment will determine the number of colored filters added to the file, which also creates the rigid perspective. Negative rigid perspectives, when reinforced multiple times, grow until they become full-fledged resentment, regardless of the personality type. When blame becomes resentment, problems are sure to follow.

Expectations are not just limited to the desire to repeat certain occasions; they can also be attached to people. As children, we expect our parents to provide for us and have all the answers to our questions. Initially those expectations are met because we have nothing to compare them to. As time goes on and we are exposed to new objects and have more experiences, we want more objects and experiences. We expect the people who started out providing the experiences and objects to continue to give us new experiences and objects. As we meet new people and hear about their experiences and see the various objects that they have, the desire to have what they have, and experience what they've experienced creeps in to our thoughts.

Depending on your childhood and your parents' ability to provide for you, your expectations might continue to be fulfilled well into early adulthood, or cease altogether because your parents didn't have the means to provide new objects and exciting experiences.

For the warrior child who wanted more but for whatever reason didn't get more, the drive to create their own experiences becomes an expectation in and of itself. For the victim child, the desire to have what others have grows stronger, but the accompanying belief that they will never have anything overpowers the desire to have it, and the feeling of powerlessness grows stronger. For both personality types, a folder that started out in the LOVE cabinet containing conclusions describing excitement, contentment and joy after receiving objects or experiences, will eventually end up in the FEAR cabinet when the expectations are not met.

Expectation placed on yourself is not really any different than expectations placed on others, except where blame is concerned. The warrior will keep trying to fulfill the expectation and not accept blame until all avenues are exhausted. This can become a pattern of self defeating behavior and continue until the mind and the physiological body can no longer deal with the stress of trying to achieve. The victim will continue to accumulate wants and needs, and assign blame to anyone and everyone when those wants and needs are not obtained. The reinforced conclusion that they are powerless to obtain things for themselves is equally as self-defeating as the warrior's pattern of behavior, it is just expressed in an opposing manner.

When your mind and your spirit are balanced, as it is when you are very young and you are living in the moment, life is easy. Once you reach the age of reasoning, which is at the same time you begin forming conclusions, life becomes more challenging.

CHAPTER 7

~Words are things. You must be careful, careful about calling people out of their names, using racial pejoratives and sexual pejoratives and all that ignorance. Don't do that. Some day we'll be able to measure the power of words. I think they are things. They get on the walls. They get in your wallpaper. They get in your rugs, in your upholstery, and your clothes, and finally in to you. ~ Maya Angelou

THE POWER OF OUR CONCLUSIONS

Words are important because they form our conclusions at our current level of understanding. The mind's process doesn't reassess the conclusions it uses as references every time your intellect advances, unless you make a point of consciously doing so. The initial understanding of a word will have a very different definition at five years of age than at fifteen or twenty-five. For example, take a moment to think of your personal definition of the word 'love' when you were five years old and compare that to your definition of the word 'love' today. Words are the things we use to communicate with ourselves, and with one another, so our use of words shapes the course of our life.

Each time an emotionally difficult or painful conclusion is referenced and reinforced, a desire to never have to experience those feelings again becomes its own thing.

When I was 10 years old, a family member began sexually molesting me. The physical sensation of his touch on my body felt good, but this person told me that what we were doing was a "big secret" and if anyone found out we would get in "big trouble." I knew that what we were doing was bad, but I was conflicted. I enjoyed the physical sensation of his touch, and I felt grown up. Most importantly, I didn't want to get in trouble. He told me that if anyone ever asked me anything about what we did when we were alone, I had to keep our secret and lie. The conclusions I formed at ten used the only words I knew and understood at the time that described the conflict I had regarding this experience. I already had a folder in my FEAR cabinet labeled WHEN I LIE I GET IN TROUBLE, so I knew that if I was caught in a lie there were consequences that would be physically and emotionally painful.

By the time I reached the age where it is natural to be curious about sex, there were discordant descriptions and feelings surrounding intimate touching and sex in my files that had been referenced and reinforced multiple times. HAVING SEX IS---------- was filed in my FEAR cabinet – not because the physical sensation and accompanying feelings felt awful, but because there was fear of getting in trouble as a result of participating in it. There was also a lot of guilt and shame for 'allowing' this person to convince me to do something he said we shouldn't be doing.

At 13 years of age, I was raped by the drunk father of children I was babysitting. The wife of this man caught him in the act. She screamed at him, "How could you do this? She's only a child!" I didn't understand at the time that I was only a child, or why these men were doing something with me that we clearly shouldn't be doing, so the conclusions I formed after these experiences were not entirely accurate. When she took me home, she begged me to keep this a secret, and I did. My perspectives as a result of these two experiences started out as: A) sex is something that *all men* just take from you, and B) having sex is something to be ashamed about. Both conclusions were far from the truth of what happened, and these conclusions shaped my future for many years.

When I reached my late teens, the fear of being caught having sex was negated by the need to exert independence and assume control of my own life. My promiscuity was my way of fighting back against those who I believed had taken something from me, and I desperately wanted to be in control of my own self. Deciding who I would give my body to was an attempt to 'show *them* who's boss.' In reality, it was a defense mechanism that created many problems in all of my relationships with men – both personally and at work – until the file was reassessed and the experience healed when I cleaned out my FEAR cabinet.

THE FILES BEING REFERENCED AREN'T ALWAYS WHAT YOU THINK

When I went through the files contained in my own FEAR cabinet during my own healing process, I learned that there was already a rigid perspective that told me that men just take what they want and were not to be trusted already filed in my FEAR cabinet. The file was labeled: BE WARY OF MEN BECAUSE---------- and already had numerous conclusions describing emotionally and physically painful experiences with the men who were present in my life. The resulting apprehension and powerlessness I originally felt towards men turned into defiance when I reached my middle teen years and started fully embracing my warrior personality type.

The conclusion that I should be ashamed of the act of sex was *added to* the folder entitled: I SHOULD BE ASHAMED OF MYSELF BECAUSE----------, which was created as a very young child after being scolded for something. The phrase 'You should be ashamed of yourself' was something I heard often as a young child when I was being disciplined.

The exact words and phrases that we used when we began forming conclusions become so engrained in our thoughts from our mind's process, that we are completely unaware of their power in our overall thoughts and in our behavior patterns until we take the time to consciously and mindfully look at them.

CONDITIONED RESPONSES BECOME FILTERS

By now, you are beginning to understand that we create patterns in our minds based on our perspectives, which were formed from our personal perceptions of our experiences. Every time we had a similar experience, the outcome – as described or outlined in our mind's folder, with all the words we used and all the emotions we felt during the experience – is reinforced multiple times. The overall pattern or outcome – the hurt feelings and the words and phrases we used to understand what happened – become a conditioned expectation when we think we are in the same situations. As mentioned earlier, this is why some people who grew up in abusive homes become abusers themselves. The conditioned expectation is a filter through which we see the world, and through which we act based on what we believe we are receiving through our hearing, sight, touch and feelings. Our filters are a two-way system. What goes out of us goes through the filter, and what comes in to us goes through the filter.

All of us are creatures of mental habit, because we lived in the same environment with the same people, so we had the same experiences with similar outcomes multiple times early on. When people – our parents, siblings, school teachers, coaches, clergy etc. – are trying to teach us things, they repeat the same phrases over and over, which include their accompanying emotions, which are themselves dependent on the perceptions, perspectives and filters through which they see the world.

As children, our feelings are easily hurt because our ability to process and interpret information is limited. When we aren't able to grasp the idea or concept our parents, siblings, school teachers, coaches, clergy etc. are trying to get across, the frustration of the 'teacher' is often interpreted negatively as criticism, which isn't pleasant, and the entire experience gets filed in the appropriate file in the FEAR cabinet with a name such as: "I CAN'T LEARN ANYTHING", or "I CAN'T DO ANYTHING RIGHT". Conclusions about our self worth become distorted.

Children do not always understand the difference between being discouraged and being condemned, and so their reactions to disappointment can sometimes be stronger than they need to be. All children understand is the feeling didn't feel good, and the person certainly appeared to be angry, so a word that they are familiar with like mad is included in the conclusion, and the word mad is associated with a feeling such as hurt or hopeless.

If the people around you didn't know any other way to express themselves except by being judgmental or critical, a pattern of recognition is set in your mind for being criticized. When other people are speaking with you and using words or phrases that you have filed in the WHEN SOMEONE IS MAD THEY ---------- folder, your mind process recognizes the pattern of criticism and concludes that they are indeed intending to hurt your feelings. Once you reach the age where you begin exerting your own personal independence, the need to defend yourself from attack becomes paramount. This defense will lead to a pattern of behavior that results in chronic conflict. Your consequent actions as the result of these filters will depend on whether you fancy yourself a warrior or are prone to avoiding confrontation. When there is no outside critic the pattern of recognition then turns inward and you become critical of yourself. This inward criticism is also a defense mechanism designed to avoid judgment from others. Additionally, you would become critical of everyone around you, not because you want to judge them, but because your patterns of recognition also become your patterns of behavior.

WHOSE PERSPECTIVE IS THE RIGHT ONE?

Words form conclusions that are ideas of that particular author – not indisputable facts.

Every single word you are reading right now expresses my opinion or my perspective which derived from my personal experiences, combined with formal education and personal studies. My opinion might not be shared by everyone, or it could be adopted by many, but either way it is still only an opinion.

Some people use sentences formed specifically for the purpose of eliciting a particular emotion or enticing a particular need in people. The advertising industry spends millions of dollars studying emotions so they can try to determine which words will provoke a specific response in the target audience. They work with psychologists, behavior analysts, and others whose job is to inform their clients which words and phrases will get people to do something specific like buy a new car or a new dress, or go on a vacation.

The way we perceive things is determined by our own personal level of awareness and our ability to understand a place, person, or thing. As you are growing and learning, you are accumulating information through all your experiences along with the definitions given to you from the people who were in your immediate surroundings – parents, teachers, older siblings, coaches, clergy, etc. Once you are old enough to reason you can make decisions, whether you realize it or not, as to whether you will accept what you have been taught or look for an alternate explanation and challenge the authority of your environment.

Challenging authority – your parents, teachers, coaches, peers, religious leaders etc. – can, and often does, create obstacles in your learning process. Some of the people you see as authority figures will welcome your curiosity and encourage you to question things, but others will be offended by it and will either try to force their supposed authority over you using shame, guilt, or by implementing some form of punishment for your insolence.

If your life isn't exactly the way you want it to be then the only way to change it is to reassess the rigid perspectives in your files. This means that you will have to challenge the authority of whoever had influence over you and contributed to the conclusions in your files.

CHAPTER 8

~ ....the knowledge of God is naturally implanted in all...~
Thomas Aquinas

OUR SIXTH SENSE

Taste, touch, smell, sight, and hearing are the senses that have been validated through scientific means. There is another sense, though, that is shared by all living creatures: intuition. This is our spirit's voice, placed inside us by the Creator of all of life – by God. Our intuition is our direct link to truth, which is God's voice.

INTUITION & DIVINE GUIDANCE

I classify intuition as a sense because it doesn't come from an intellectual thought process. It completely bypasses the part of the mind that needs to arrive at a conclusion, and relays information to the part of the mind that is unbiased. You know the information is right because you feel it deep within yourself, in the center of your being.

It's that feeling that you get that you can't explain when you meet someone that you immediately don't like but can't intellectually explain why. It's the feeling of impending doom that keeps you safe from harm. It is information that is part of your spirit's knowledge, and information channeled through your spirit from the Holy Spirit. It's those big 'Aha!' moments that reach you at the core of your being and open your heart just a little more. Intuition is Divine Guidance because our spirit is always connected to the Divine. I know that Divine Guidance is real because I have experienced it many times, and so have you! Learning to accept it for what it is and not be afraid of it is another story.

When we are young children there is no conscious wall that keeps us from communicating with our higher power or God, so it's something that every child does until they believe that they can't. Before a child is taught to be afraid of their intuition or dismiss it outright, they trust the information they receive implicitly. When a person accepts their spirit's guidance, it allows them to utilize that information when making decisions.

Children might have an 'invisible friend' or 'guardian angel' (so-named by their caregivers). Some people might even believe that there is a ghost the child is communicating with – a relative perhaps, who has passed and has gone to heaven. It is only when someone who is seen as an authority figure – one or both parents, a teacher or religious leader – challenges the validity of this communication in such a way as to suggest we should be fearful of it or dismisses it outright that we become embarrassed about communicating with something we can't intellectually understand or explain. When doubt, shame, or guilt creeps in, that form of communication is abandoned altogether.

Some children are told that only a certain, select people – such as heads of organized religious orders – are allowed to communicate with information from the unseen, which infers the power only communicates with those who are deemed worthy of it. Others are taught that the only god that anyone should have faith in is that of science. In the quest to validate everything from a scientific perspective, the ability to use and follow an internal guidance system that can't be proven has come into question, and has been ridiculed and abandoned. This need to prove everything beyond a reasonable doubt started the separation between us, the importance of ritual, and a relationship with God.

As children, we come into this world knowing, accepting, and communicating with a higher power we already know is no threat and something we can trust completely. We may not be able to explain what it is, but we know it's safe. It is only when someone else's doubts or instruction finds its way into our thoughts, do we start to question communication with our higher power. The more this communication is questioned, belittled, criticized, or made fun of, the less likely we will be willing to communicate with it.

THE INVISIBLE INTELLIGENCE
& THE HOLY SPIRIT

There is an invisible field of intelligence that surrounds us. Inside this intelligence field are the answers to every question you could think of. The intelligence in this field is made up of all of those who came before us – our ancestors. This invisible intelligence has been given different names by the people who accept it and regularly communicate with it, the most common being guardian angels, spirit guides, and the Holy Spirit. Over the years there have been many other names assigned to this field of intelligence, but the name isn't as important as the belief in its existence, and the understanding of how it works.

People outside of religious orders who have nurtured their ability to communicate with this intelligence are often ostracized, ridiculed, and publicly shamed. Some people are labeled with a disease and institutionalized, so it's no wonder that when a person hears messages they will deny them.

Some people are content to be in the fringes of mainstream society and use a combination of intuition and worldly tools to not only understand themselves what is going on in their own life, but to also to help others. Astrologists, numerologists, clairvoyants, and tarot card readers are often called frauds, hucksters, or con artists. While it is true that some of these folks are taking advantage of people and are conning them out of their money and are frauds, there are others who really do have a solid understanding of their craft and an open line with the collective unconscious or angel realm. Some of these folks are genuinely helping others come to terms with their life experiences, and some are undoubtedly creating more havoc in the lives of those who seek their counsel.

Artists – writers, musicians, painters, sculptors, actors, film makers, and photographers – are another group of people that often receive inspiration from the field and pass their message on through their art.

Sometimes though, when you feel stuck, a peek into the unknown might be all it takes to inch you forward. Remember, the field will gently guide you to where you need to be whether it's you that taps into it, or another person that taps into it for you. You are already receiving guidance through the field all the time anyway, you are likely just dismissing it or thinking that your own mind came up with the guidance. Divine messages come through conversations with a friend, or in a song, or even from a character in a TV show or movie. Divine guidance can come from anywhere because the field literally surrounds us.

Learning to once again connect with our higher power through our spirit and trust the guidance you receive through your intuition is part of the process of healing, and the return to remembering who and what you really are. Love and fear cannot inhabit the same space at the same time, so if you are still reacting to things that people say in a defensive manner or blaming people in your life for things that have happened, your internal guidance system must work harder to be heard.

SECTION II –
THE PATH TO HEALING

CHAPTER 9

~The most important relationship we can all have is the one you have with yourself; the most important journey you can take is one of self discovery. To know yourself, you must spend time with yourself, you must not be afraid to be alone. Knowing yourself is the beginning of all wisdom. ~Aristotle

PERSPECTIVES BECOME PROBLEMS

Memory is nothing more than stored information – data that our mind accesses to help us understand what we are experiencing in the present.

We begin an experience, our mind looks inside the filing cabinet for a file that contains a word or phrase that best describes what we are seeing, smelling tasting, touching, and hearing. The files with the most colored filters are the ones referenced more often, because those are the files that determine whether we will have a similar experience, or whether we will immediately begin a pattern of behavior that has proven itself to be one that helps us avoid that kind of experience.

Remember, problems are the result of unmet expectations, and expectations are nothing more than files that have been referenced and reinforced multiple times. So if you want fewer problems in your life, you'll need to understand how those expectations developed. Once you understand where your perspectives came from, you can then choose, using your current level of understanding, whether those perspectives and expectations are still relevant, or if they can now be tossed out. The FEAR cabinet is so named for a reason. There is scary stuff in there! It is a cabinet full of unpleasant memories, and revisiting those files is going to take some doing.

You're going to need help reassessing and resolving the information contained in your files, and the kind of help I'm talking about comes from something that you can't see, touch, smell, or taste. The kind of help I'm talking about comes from the intelligence and wisdom of the collective unconscious – the Holy Spirit. This help speaks directly to your spirit and fosters a reconnection from your Spirit to God.

How will you know when the Divine is speaking to you? You'll feel it. You'll know the information is coming from something other than your own mind, because 1) it will be without any judgment, and 2) you'll feel a sensation deep inside yourself at the holiest of altars, where the light of God resides inside you.

Reconnecting to your spirit takes practice, and everyone has their own way of connecting. There are many types of meditation you can try, or you may find that you connect with your spirit through listening to music, journaling, walking, running, doing yoga, sculpting, or painting. Remember, you'll know when you've connected because you'll feel it.

When you are ready to dig into your FEAR cabinet and learn the truth of your painful experiences, ask God to guide you to the truth. You must be ready and willing to receive the truth otherwise, you'll end up reinforcing the perspectives that are creating all the problems in your life once again.

~Cultivate the root; the leaves and the branches will take care of themselves.
~ Confucius

WORD CONNOTATIONS & TRIGGERS

Many things contribute to our personal connotation of a word. People who have experienced physical or emotional trauma are often triggered by a specific word or phrase, smell, or sound. When you consider words, smells and sounds are filed together in the same folder, it becomes easier to understand the concept of triggers, and the power that they can have over you.

The first step in understanding how you interpret things, or the way you perceive things and file them away is to think about how you use and understand the words that are in your conclusions. Now, it's important to understand that not every word in your entire vocabulary will have an emotion attached to it or be a trigger or a problem. Some words are merely descriptions of people, places or things, but you will have key words which will have intense emotions attached to them, because these are the words you use to describe the emotionally painful experiences.

START A HEALING NOTEBOOK OR JOURNAL

You may want to get a notebook or hardcover journal to jot down thoughts and answers to specific questions we will consider in this section.

First, we will take a look at how you personally interpret or understand words. This list contains some words that may be attached to strong emotions, while other words on this list might be considered neutral, and are not attached to any emotions. There are no right or wrong answers to anything in this section. You are the only one inside your mind, so you are the only one with answers to you.

Each person can only understand things from their own perceptions and perspectives, so there is a strong likelihood that a lot of words that may hold meaning for you are missing off this list. If reading through this list causes you to think of other words that have importance to you, please jot those words down in your journal, and then consider the questions at the bottom of the list when thinking about those words.

~In the beginning was the word, and the word was with God,
and the word was God~ John 1:1

EXERCISE
PART 1 — WORDS

Read the following list of words slowly and pay close attention to the feeling or emotion you feel as you read them.

Love	Wound	Nurtured	Touched
Blamed	Bad	Dismissed	Violated
Punishment	Stung	Authority	Scary
Masturbate	Torture	Intercourse	Rape
Minister	Priest	Rabbi	Imam
Violence	Betrayed	Sex	Entitled

CONSIDER THE FOLLOWING:
As you read through the list, which word(s) generated a feeling?

_____

_____

_____

Was that feeling positive or negative?

_____

Were you embarrassed by any of the words? If so, which ones and why do you think you were you embarrassed? Who taught you the word?

_____

_____

_____

_____

Did any word cause a memory to come to mind? What was the memory? What are your feelings associated with that memory?

_____

_____

_____

_____

Were there words that were neutral – or didn't generate any kind of feeling for you? Which words were they?

_____

_____

_____

PART 2 - FEELINGS

Feelings are the result or the consequence of our perceptions. Feelings are not right or wrong, they are what they are at the time. When we understand why we perceive things the way we do, we can create situations that will provide us with the feelings we prefer to have.

Beside each of the following emotions or feelings, write down five words that you associate with the feeling. Pay attention to the thoughts that come to you as you read each word and how your body is affected as you say each word.

FURIOUS _____

ASHAMED _____

EXCITED _____

STRESSED _____

GUILTY _____

HOPEFUL _____

DEPRESSED _____

HATE _____

AFRAID _____

HAPPY _____

Did you smile or laugh out loud as you thought of words to put beside certain feelings?

_____

Did you heart rate increase or decrease as you thought of words you associated with negative feelings?

_____

Did your face flush?

_____

Did you think of any feelings that weren't part of this list, but are meaningful to you?

_____

_____

The level of power a word carries varies from person to person and is completely dependent on the feelings they attached to the conclusions they formed in their mind and filed away. Each time a conclusion was reinforced, the level of power attached to the conclusion becomes more intense.

PHRASES, SENTENCES AND PERSPECTIVES

Words come together to form phrases, and phrases form the conclusions that are filed in the folders in the filing cabinets of your mind.

Some phrases are associated with an image or a universal story you were told that was intended to convey a specific message.

He/she is down-to-earth
He is a dirty old man
Let go and let God

These are a dime a dozen
Don't rain on my parade
This is a piece of cake
Quit beating around the bush
Don't cry wolf
You're making a mountain out of a mole hill
I'm between a rock and a hard place
I'm on cloud nine
Curiosity killed the cat
Don't look a gift horse in the mouth

Put a ✔ beside the phrases you recognized.

How many of these phrases have you said yourself?

_____

What does each phrase mean to you?

_____

_____

_____

_____

_____

_____

_____

_____

_____

CHAPTER 10

~The miracle [of healing] is possible when cause and consequence
are brought together, not kept separate
~ Helen Schucman, A Course in Miracles

DISCOVER YOUR PERSPECTIVES
BY WRITING IN A JOURNAL

Your perspectives are the consequence of your experiences. Just like experiences come and go, so too can your perspectives about them. In reviewing and reassessing your perspectives, you are really just getting to know yourself better!

After completing the word, phrase and feelings sections, you probably have a pretty good idea of the wording you used for your conclusions, and which words hold power for you. Remember, it isn't usually the good feeling experiences that go on to create problems in your life, it's the emotionally painful experiences that affect your life in a negative way. No one wants to relive a painful past, but the only way to truly heal from these experiences is to understand them.

Journaling is a safe and private way to begin going through your FEAR cabinet. It's beneficial to review what you've written in your journal from time to time, so you can see how much progress you're making.

To get started cleaning out your FEAR cabinet, ask yourself the following questions:

1. What are the three most emotionally painful experiences that immediately come to mind?
2. What age were you when you had each experience?
3. What are the conclusions you arrived at for each experience?
4. Who are the people involved in these experiences and what were their roles?
5. What makes you angry/sad/fearful about each experience?

As you write down each experience, be as detailed as possible with each question. For example: what do you recall these people saying or doing during this experience? How did their words and actions make you feel?

Review each experience as objectively as you can by asking yourself:

1. Was I old enough to properly assess the situation?
2. Did I really know the motives of the people I believe hurt me?
3. Is it possible that I misread the motives of the people involved?
4. How would I react today?
5. What did I learn from this experience?

Once you have finished reassessing the first three painful experiences that came to your mind, write down three more and go through the entire process again and again and again! Every so often, go back to the beginning of your journal and read through the experiences and conclusions you recalled. Can you see a recurring theme or pattern in your experiences?

~ Children cannot grow to psychological maturity in an atmosphere of unpredictability, haunted by the specter of abandonment
~ Dr. M. Scott Peck

ALL WOUNDS DEVELOP IN CHILDHOOD

There are some emotional wounds that are common among all human beings. These are sometimes referred to as 'archetypal' wounds. Every person has, of course, had their own unique experiences in life, so although there are common wounds, the specific way the wound was inflicted is not.

Commonalities in human behavior are referred to as archetypes. As noted in the book *The Wisdom of Carl Jung*, Dr. Jung explained archetypes as patterns of thought that are universal among all of mankind. He referred to these common patterns as the collective unconscious and is quoted as saying, "Below our personal unconscious lies an incredibly, almost unfathomably, deep realm that all humanity shares." All humanity. It is important to understand that everyone faces challenges in life regardless of their circumstances.

Every person in every culture experiences, and can recognize in others, a host of similar emotions through body language and facial expressions, although what causes a person to feel a specific emotion is unique to them. In his book *Emotions Revealed*, Psychologist Dr. Paul Ekman explains in detail how people from all over the world recognize emotions such as anger, joy, and sadness in the faces of others.

Similar patterns of thought lead to similar emotions in all people. Wounds are wounds regardless of their labels. Whether these types of wounds are classified as archetypal, or just accepted as conditions of the human experience shouldn't really matter as much as how a person finds a way to heal from them.

Being left alone, ostracized, and isolated from one's family or community is a universal fear and can create a deep emotional wound – an archetypal wound of abandonment.

Dr. Mario Martinez, in his book *The Mind Body Code*, tells us there are three emotional archetypal wounds: abandonment, shame, and betrayal. He explains that these wounds are consistent across cultures even though the precise nature of how a person perceives being abandoned, shamed or betrayed is unique to each person. Abandonment, Dr. Martinez asserts, disempowers us because it breaks a pledge. A child assumes the pledge of commitment from their parent, and the idea of abandonment from a child's perspective is very different than from an adult's perspective.

I was adopted as a child and some psychologists would argue that the very act of being put up for adoption itself would create an abandonment wound. For me, I believe that being left alone in a hospital in a different city when I was only ten had more to do with feelings of abandonment than being put up for adoption (although I did, from time to time, wonder why I was given up for adoption in the first place).

It's important to understand that just because a doctor, psychologist, or book states a supposed fact about an emotional issue, it doesn't necessarily make it the truth for you. Each of us experiences things in our own way, and we feel things in our own personal way. You are the only person who has lived your life, so you are the only one that really knows the how's and why's of you.

For instance, a person who grows up in a home where there is a great deal of emotional and physical abuse will downplay the level of abuse they suffered as a child to themselves and others, because their life experience conditioned them to accept the abuse as normal, compared to a person who never experienced abuse as a child.

COMPASSION, KINDESS, AND GOD'S MESSENGERS

Although our memories tend to highlight the negative and downright scary things filed in our minds, there are usually glimpses of light filed in the same memory as well. It might be one sentence in that memory, but it will be there. Glimpses of light might appear in the form of someone who showed kindness or who provided emotional tools that were important for the situation that we were in. We are always given exactly what we need to get through a situation, and once we learn to recognize that God was and still is always with us, our abandonment, betrayal, and other issues are easily healed.

Once you make the decision to change your life and commit to that change, you have heard the call of your spirit. When you invite the wisdom of the Holy Spirit into your life, and are ready to accept the truth, your healing will begin. This wisdom might come to you when you write in your journal, or when you sit in silent meditation. There are no rules relating to how the wisdom of all of those who came before will come to you. It is easier, of course, to hear the guidance when you can silence your mind, so you have to find a way to stop the constant chatter in your mind that reminds you of all the reasons that you should stay angry and isolated from your true self. Go for a walk, jog, ride a bike, go for a hike outside the city, take up yoga or Tai Chi. Do whatever it takes to silence your mind and then listen. Remember, you'll know when you've received Divine Guidance, because it will be wisdom without judgment.

WHAT GOES AROUND COMES AROUND

The filters that are created in our minds are two-way filters. We not only receive other people's energy in the form of communication through these filters, but we send out our own energy via various communication methods through them as well. Our actions are the result of our true beliefs, so if we believe that we have been abused, maligned, bullied, taken advantage of, or victimized, we will do what we can to protect ourselves, and in doing so, unintentionally, and unconsciously send out negative energy into the universe. When we are in a negative energy field, we are likely to inflict some emotional and possibly even physical wounds on others.

The idea that we get back what we put out into the universe is referred to as the law of attraction or karma, and some people understand these phrases to mean that the universe or God will punish those who step out of line. The misunderstanding comes from the idea that 'bad' people will 'get what's coming to them', and that the universe will make sure that happens. This stems from the belief that God, the father or ruler of the universe, will punish the wicked. This belief comes from a place of fear rather than truth. God does not punish. The universe does not punish. People punish, and people seek punishment to validate their emotional pain.

The universe responds to the energy of the truth of our being, not what we think we think. Who and what we believe we are, is determined by what we believe we have experienced, which is based on the conclusions our young mind arrived at before we were old enough to comprehend the truth. The law of attraction then, is responding to the rigid perspectives that are being referenced, and when our FEAR cabinet contains more rigid perspectives than our LOVE cabinet, we are putting out the very energy that we are trying to avoid. When we think we are intending to affect change in our life by choosing positive thoughts, but we stay stuck in the muck of the truth of our life, we become frustrated, angry, and resentful. What is really happening is we are misunderstanding how energy is communicated throughout the universe.

FORGIVENESS IS THE ONLY
WAY PASSED THE PAIN

Suppose someone says something to you that hurts your feelings. You are immediately taken aback, you feel a sinking feeling in the pit of your stomach, your face flushes and you can feel your hands start to tremble. Your mind – in a microsecond – has gone into the filing cabinets of your mind, retrieved a similar experience and put the conclusion you arrived at in the forefront of your mind. Before you have time to consciously recognize that old memory from what you are currently experiencing, your mind has already arrived at the same conclusion, and added this current experience to the original folder. The person who hurt your feelings in this instant is put in the same mind folder as the person in the past, and you have reinforced an old conclusion. Your reaction to this current experience and person will be a mixture of the old hurt feelings with the new. Your mind has brought your past into your present and depending on how you choose to respond to this person, your future may also be affected.

In the Lord's Prayer, we ask God to 'forgive us our trespasses, as we forgive those who trespass against us.' The importance of forgiveness has been around for as long as people have been around, because people make mistakes. No one is perfect but before you are going to be able to forgive someone else for the wounds you believe they inflicted on you, you are going to have to take a good long look at yourself first. We can only give the things to others that we own for ourselves; unless we own our own mistakes and forgive ourselves for those mistakes, any attempt at forgiving someone else will be disingenuous.

Forgiveness really does set you free. True forgiveness heals the emotional wounds you carry around in the conclusions your mind arrived at that are stored in your FEAR cabinet. You will know when the wound contained in one of these files is healed and the perceived perpetrators forgiven when you genuinely feel an affinity with and toward them. This can only happen when you allow the wisdom of the Holy Spirit to shine light on the darkness contained in your files.

CHAPTER 11

OUR SPIRIT IS OUR CONSCIENCE

~Why do you see the speck in your neighbor's eye, but you do not notice the log in your own eye? Or, how can you say to your neighbor, friend, let me take out the speck in your eye when you yourself do not see the log in your own eye? You hypocrite, first take the log out of your own eye, and then you will see clearly to take the speck out of your neighbor's eye. ~ Jesus talking about judging others, according to Luke 6:39

Before you can forgive yourself, you must first admit to the things you know you've done that were wrong but justified to yourself and everyone else. Everyone knows when they've done something they shouldn't have. There's a feeling you get, in the same place in the middle of your body – in your gut – where you have felt your own hurt – that signals to you that you've said or done something that you shouldn't have. The consequence is a feeling of guilt, and everyone feels guilt at some point, because everyone has said or done something that hurt someone else. Sometimes a person's emotions become so out of control they physically hurt someone. It happens. If you are honest with yourself, I'm sure you can recall a time where you slapped someone in anger or punched or kicked someone. Or perhaps you lied but convinced yourself that you were just in your lies. Maybe you've manipulated someone in some way to get something that you wanted and convinced yourself that you had to do whatever it was you did because the outcome was a necessity.

Confessing one's transgressions doesn't have to take place between two people but looking someone else in the eyes and admitting to the things you've done that hurt others generates a level of honesty that might not present itself otherwise. If you know someone that you can trust to receive what you are going to tell them without judgment – great! If you don't – that's ok too. Start a new page or section in your journal and begin.

1. Write down three things that you have done that were mean, awful, judgmental, selfish or harmful in some way to another human being.
2. Describe why you believe you behaved the way you did, paying attention to the specific goal you had. In other words, what was it that you believed you would gain from hurting the feelings (or physically) of that other person?
3. If you were to find yourself in the same situation today, do you believe that you would behave the same way?
4. What did you learn from each experience?
5. Do you believe that you have a solid understanding of your perspectives and how those perspectives caused you to behave in this way toward others?
6. Are you able to now, to see how those you thought intentionally hurt you were and are no different than you?

Are you ready to forgive your own self, which opens the door to forgive others?

As before, once you have assessed the first three transgressions that came to your mind, write down three more, and three more until you can't think of any more. With each transgression that you confess to your journal, and to God, the burden of guilt will begin to leave your body. When you feel compassion for yourself, you will eventually arrive at an understanding of those who you thought had intentionally harmed you and extend compassion towards them. When you can understand and feel compassion toward yourself, you can understand and feel compassion toward others. Understanding and compassion are the first steps in knowing unconditional love.

~How deluded we sometimes are by the clear notions we get out of books. They make us think we really understand things of which we have no practical knowledge at all.~ Thomas Merton

I know how hard it is to work through years of emotional pain and trauma. I've been there, done that, and been there and done that again and again and again! I worked with a counselor and attended group sessions for several years until I slowly gained my strength back. I thought that was all I needed to do, and that my life would just go along tickity-boo now that I had regained some sense of self.

I quit going to counseling and to group, and slowly slipped backwards into resentment, bitterness, and anger. When my life reached an unacceptable level of miserable again, I would go to church or book an appointment with a counselor or psychologist, and when I felt better – I would stop going, and I would slip backwards again. I read every self-help book that called out to me, and I kept trying to heal. I journaled and journaled until I felt that I had gotten rid of all the anger, bitterness and resentment that I had been carrying for decades. When I was ready to heal, I felt the presence of something Holy come into my being. I was so overjoyed, I giggled like I did when I was a little kid. I thought that I was there. That I had finally learned all I needed to know, and I was finally done! Then, my brother died by suicide, and I took a huge step backwards.

All the anger that I thought I had let go of returned and filled my body. I felt betrayed by God. I did everything that I thought I was supposed to do, and I slipped backwards so fast that I couldn't even believe it! I became physically sick. My body had had enough, and it broke. I had never been this ill before, and that seemed to break me even further. I was physically, emotionally, and spiritually drained and I wanted to die. I wanted the pain and the punishment to end.

I finally made the decision to be rid of all of it once and for all. I told God that I was tired and that I couldn't live my life like this for one more second! The pain had to stop once and for all and I needed to know how to make it stop for good. I told God that I needed guidance and I needed it now, otherwise I would rather die. He pointed me in the direction that I needed to go, and I studied and journaled some more, I spoke with a psychologist, and I prayed until I felt all the anger, resentment and bitterness leave my body. The yuck that I had been carrying around in my FEAR cabinet was replaced with Divine Truth – an understanding and compassion for myself and for all those who I believed had intentionally harmed me. Painful memories were put into storage, and my mind started to dig into my LOVE cabinet more often. I received the Grace I asked for, because I was finally ready to receive it. Healing is a process that will take as long as it takes, and it starts with your willingness.

For a lot of years, I pretended that the emotionally and physically painful things that happened in my life didn't have any affect on me, but they did. Of course they did, because after each experience I told myself a story about what happened. I formed a conclusion, and my mind referenced those conclusions over and over and over again throughout my life. It wasn't until I finally said enough! It was time to clean out my FEAR cabinet once and for all and return to my natural state of being – one of wonder, joy and contentment. Do I still get angry? Of course. I'm still human. Do I still find old wounds that haven't been healed yet? Of course. I've lived over a half of a century, and I've had millions of experiences and created millions of files.

I've broken down one of my early childhood experiences explaining the process of how my initial perception led to rigid perspectives, and how those rigid perspectives created problems in my life. I hope that by reading through the healing process of this experience, you are encouraged to travel back in your own memories and understand how your early painful experiences had an impact on your own life. My hope is that by sharing the steps I took, I can provide you with the tools of how to begin your own process of healing and find the same joy, contentment and peace that I have.

CHAPTER 12

FROM PAIN TO TRUTH

I was born with a skeletal deformity that required multiple orthopedic surgeries for me to be pain free and to keep walking. The physical and emotional trauma from this one experience was referenced in my mind for decades, influenced many decisions and created solidified perspectives that I held on to well into my adult life. These rigid perspectives shaped who I thought I was for many years and contributed to many difficult and combative interactions with others. That's how it works. Remember, the filters of our perspectives go both ways. The mind processes information so quickly we are often unaware of where our opinions originated, or how many experiences are referenced at the same time that we arrive at a decision.

MY FIRST SURGERY

My father took me to see his chiropractor when I was around 9 years old. Shortly after arriving in the office, his attendant put me into a private room and asked me to change into a backless medical gown. She said she would come and get me when the doctor was ready to see me. I remember feeling anxious, although I couldn't explain why. I already knew that I was 'different', and I also knew that being different wasn't a good thing. When I walked, my legs didn't move forward in a straight line; instead, they rotated in a circular motion. With each step I took, my pelvis would fall creating an exaggerated limp. Adults would stare at me with a look of pity of their face when they saw me walk, and some of the kids at school had already started teasing me. I was the 'weebles wobble and don't fall down' kid.

When it was my turn to see the doctor, I had barely entered the room when he announced: "Oh oh! This is way beyond my capabilities. She needs to see an orthopedic surgeon." He told my dad that an x-ray would confirm what he could tell just by looking at me, and it did. Pointing to the x-ray displayed on the viewer, he explained that I had something called hip dysplasia in both of my hips, the left side being worse than the right. It meant I was lacking the socket part of the hip, so my femur (leg bone) was basically floating beside the pelvis instead of sitting inside a proper joint, and this was the reason that I limped so badly. He suggested my dad contact our family doctor and ask for a referral to an orthopedist.

MY PERCEPTION

When I first brought this memory to the forefront of my mind I recalled most of the details, but not all of them. Memory is not always as reliable as we think it is. I remember that I felt afraid, even though I hadn't had any similar experiences that would have indicated I should be afraid. I knew I was afraid, so my mind had located the folder entitled I AM AFRAID BECAUSE ---------- and found a reference. Eventually, I would learn what was in the folder that was referenced.

Not knowing what is going to happen and feeling anxious as a result is normal, but no one knew to explain it to me in exactly that way. I doubt that anyone even thought they needed to. The idea that I was different had to have been referenced many times before, because those words stuck out in my memory. I understood that the folder labelled I AM DIFFERENT BECAUSE ---------- was filed in my FEAR cabinet because of the negative emotions attached to it. The looks and stares from other kids, as well as adults, validated my belief that they all thought I was different, so the negative connotation associated with this word was already reinforced multiple times. From this point on, every time the word 'different' was used in any context, I was going to feel an added apprehension that didn't necessarily need to be there.

The conversation going on inside my 10-year-old head was something like:

1. That nurse was nice, and she talked to me kind of like my mom does
2. The x-ray machine room is cold and the people using the machines are wearing big, black, heavy aprons. The people told me they had to wear big heavy aprons to protect themselves and that is kind of scary.
3. The doctor is angry because he's talking really loud and he looks upset.

The conclusions I arrived at were:

1. Women are comforting – filed in my LOVE cabinet
2. X-rays are dangerous – filed in my FEAR cabinet
3. Doctors are scary – filed in my FEAR cabinet

My FEAR cabinet was already collecting more folders than my LOVE cabinet during this experience, and the experience was just beginning.

Being only 10 years old, my vocabulary was limited, so the words I used to describe this event in my folder were already attached to certain emotions. The female nurse's caring treatment was immediately referenced in the LOVE cabinet, and the folder chosen was the one that associated caring with Mom. This reinforced the idea in my mind that Mom = caring. I was beginning to form an expectation that all women were moms, and that all moms were caring and loving. This expectation was reinforced for decades, until I met a mother who was so emotionally wounded as a child, she couldn't even begin to be caring or loving, because she was so desperate to be loved herself. Her children had never been nurtured or cared for, so they had no idea how to be emotionally engaged in their own personal relationships.

The male doctor's voice was loud, and I thought I saw a scowl on his face. The sound of his voice and what I believed was a scowl caused my mind to retrieve a file with a conclusion in it that said he was angry. That file was placed forefront of my mind, and I arrived at the conclusion that the doctor must have been angry because he spoke in a similar manner and he wasn't smiling. As soon as the doctor said, "This is beyond me," my senses picked up on the fear in the room, so my own fear intensified. My initial perception that this was going to be scary was confirmed, a conclusion beginning with I AM AFRAID BECAUSE ---------- was completed with "the doctor was angry with me and didn't know what to do to fix me."

My dad arranged an appointment with an orthopedic surgeon through our family doctor immediately after returning home that day. I remember sitting across from the surgeon, a big oak desk between us. There were pictures of his family on the desk and a lot of diplomas hanging on the wall. The room seemed huge and I felt small in comparison, and uncomfortable. On the desk behind him, an x-ray viewer held images of my pelvis and hip joints.

This doctor didn't mince words or try to paint an optimistic picture; he simply stated the facts as he understood them. He told us the only thing that could help me was a type of surgery that he himself could not perform. He didn't know of anyone in Saskatchewan that could, and if we could find someone to do the surgery, he believed that I would be in a full body cast afterward for at least 6 months. He didn't know what the outcome would be, but he did believe that if I didn't have some kind of surgery I would be in a wheelchair by the time I turned 14. My dad was so shaken by this news he let out a gasp which started a huge wave of fear in me and I started to cry hysterically. We both left that office feeling terrified and hopeless. Ironically, I would eventually come to have tremendous love and respect for this surgeon and his matter of fact way of presenting things.

Hearing similar words from this doctor (this is beyond me), seeing and hearing the panicked response from my dad, and feeling the gravity of my situation based on the tone of the voices and the reactions my mind interpreted from what I was seeing, caused my mind to add a conclusion to the existing folder labeled: I AM AFRAID BECAUSE---------- filed in the front of the drawer in the FEAR cabinet. Although I had no real concept of what being in a wheelchair for life meant, I knew it wasn't what I or anyone else wanted.

The conversation going on inside my head was something like:

1. I am going to be in a wheelchair for the rest of my life and this is really scary

2. No one can help me because I am different
3. No one knows what to do to fix this
4. Doctors are really scary people

The conclusions I arrived at were:

1. No one knows what to do – filed in my FEAR cabinet
2. Doctors are scary – reinforced, validated & a colored filter added to reflect the level of fear associated with doctors. Re-filed in FEAR cabinet

My parents owned and operated a small neighborhood hardware store. I was helping in the store one Saturday when a regular customer came in. He belonged to the local Wa Wa Shrine Temple and knew of the rare work done in many Shrine Hospitals in North America. He asked me why I walked "that way," and if I had been in an accident. I remember feeling embarrassed, awkward, and full of shame even though this man seemed concerned, as though he wanted to help. After speaking with my dad and learning about my situation, he arranged for us to see an orthopedic surgeon at the Shriner's Hospital in Winnipeg. My parents were given the hope they wanted.

At this appointment, I was sent for more x-rays of my hips as well as x-rays of my feet. I hadn't ever had x-rays of my feet, and the first two doctors hadn't said anything about anything being wrong with my feet. This doctor seemed to be more concerned more about the high arch of my foot than the problem with my hips, and I was confused. I started to wonder what was really wrong with me.

My parents grew up in a time where doctors were placed atop a pedestal and were never to be questioned. They also had limited medical understanding, so when the surgeon convinced them that fixing my feet would ultimately correct my hip condition, they believed him.

My surgery was booked in the summer so I wouldn't miss any school. My whole family piled into our station wagon, and off to Winnipeg we went. It was about a six-hour drive from our home in Regina. My brother and sister were several years older than I was and had also been adopted as babies. We were all singing songs in the back of the car, behaving as if we were going on vacation. I knew I was going for surgery, but I didn`t really know what that meant. It had been explained to me that they were going to cut me open and fix my feet, and that is exactly how I understood it.

As we drove down Portage Ave. on our way to Winnipeg Children`s Hospital where the surgery would take place, the reality of what was going to happen was starting to sink in. They were going to cut my feet open. They were going to CUT MY FEET OPEN! The more I thought about them cutting my feet open, the more I became overwhelmed by fear and I started to cry. My mom tried to comfort me telling me it will be ok, but my dad quickly became frustrated. He told me to quit being a baby and to stop crying immediately. I was so scared that I could feel my heart pounding inside my chest. I thought it would burst right open. The pounding inside my chest scared me as much as my dad yelling at me to stop crying, and as much as the anticipation of what was going to happen to me. I cried uncontrollably.

We arrived at the hospital and after a little while, a person dressed in a white uniform showed us to my room. I remember seeing a lot of different kids with various deformities and illnesses as we walked down the hallway. I was holding my mom`s hand and still sobbing as we made our way towards the room I was going to be in. My dad was quick to point out all the kids that were much worse than I was, and told me that what I would be having done was not nearly as big as what they were facing, and told me I should be ashamed of myself for carrying on like a baby.

I had no real idea what my dad's motivations were or what the truth was as to why he would be saying all those things or scolding me so much. All I knew at the time is what I could see, hear, touch, smell and feel. My 10-year-old brain interpreted the comments my dad said to me during the drive to the hospital and the walk down the hallway to my room and referenced the words that hurt my feelings against words that had been spoken to me in previously filed experiences.

The conversation going on inside my head was something like:

1. Every time I cry when I'm scared, I get yelled at.

2. These kids are worse off than I am, so they must be more important than me.
3. I should be ashamed of myself for crying and behaving like a baby.

The conclusions I arrived at were:

1. Crying is bad, and I'm crying, so I am bad.
2. I'm not important enough

As a child, we cannot differentiate between the feelings people around us are having due to the situation, or whether the feelings they are having are the result of something to do with us. Children read the energy they feel and interpret it at their current level of understanding. Things are black and white, and the way the mind processes the data is entirely dependant on the level of comprehension. The reality of the situation will be very different when assessed from an adult perspective.

Inside my hospital room there was a recliner, a TV mounted on the wall, and big comfy chairs beside the bed. This being a hospital dedicated to children, and understanding that children feel safer when their parents are close by, the staff encouraged my parents to stay overnight.

A nurse obtained my medical history from my parents, and a little while later the anesthesiologist came in to my room to explain how they would put me to sleep. He had a different nurse with him, and they used puppets to demonstrate what would happen in the operating room. I remember feeling that these people did not intend to hurt me and I calmed down a bit. A little while later, a different nurse came into the room carrying a tray full of vials and announced she was there to take blood. I remember thinking that if she was going to fill all those tubes, I wouldn't have any blood left! I became afraid and started to cry. The nurse could see what I was thinking and explained that she was only going to take two vials of blood from me.

My parents didn`t stay too long after that, although I`m certain that if my dad had allowed her to my mom would have gladly stayed with me the entire night and slept in the recliner. We had lived in Winnipeg for a few years just after I was adopted, so my family went to visit our old neighbors.

After they left, I lay there in that bed hearing every sound that was coming from the hallway. Every once in a while, I would peek out the door to see what was going on, then rush back to my bed before anyone saw me peeking. I was so scared of getting caught snooping and getting in trouble that I decided I should just watch TV until I fell asleep. I had been in enough trouble for one day.

Hospitals are rarely quiet, especially during the evenings and overnight. As much as I tried to go to sleep, I was afraid of what they were going to do to me the next morning, afraid of all the sounds I didn't recognize, and afraid of going through this whole thing alone.

At some point in the evening, the daughter of the neighbors that my parents were visiting with came to visit. She came with her boyfriend after attending the local fair where they had won a big stuffed frog. She felt sorry for me, so she brought the frog up to the hospital hoping that it would bring me a little comfort. I was so grateful for that frog. I remember crying again when they went to leave. She comforted me the best she could, and then they left. I held on to that frog all night, and I eventually fell asleep.

The conversation going on in my head was something like:

1. This hospital is scary
2. I'm afraid of being cut open but if I cry, I'll get in trouble
3. Why did everyone just leave me here by myself? Was it because I was bad?
4. I shouldn't have cried so much and now I'm all alone

The conclusions I arrived at were:

1. Crying is bad, and I'm crying so I am bad. Referenced, reinforced, validated, and a colored filter added. The conclusion is re-filed in my FEAR cabinet
2. I am all alone

In the morning a nurse came to my room to start an IV. She told me that it would feel kind of like a bee sting and it hurt a lot. I did my best not to cry, but it hurt so much that I did. A little while later a porter came to my room and helped me onto a gurney, and we started our journey to the operating room. There, I was moved from the gurney on to a cold stainless-steel table. A mask was placed over my mouth and nose. I was told to take slow deep breaths and count backwards from 10. I was told that I would smell something like garlic and made it to about 7 before I was fast asleep.

I woke in a large room with lots of hospital beds, groggy, and unable to lift my legs off the bed. I had heavy casts on both feet that went from my toes to my knees, and my feet felt odd. The heaviness, combined with the effects of all the anesthetic, made me weak and prevented me from bringing my knees to my chest as I usually did when I woke from a sleep. I sat up, tried to focus my eyes to see why my feet felt odd, and saw that my feet were wrapped in white stuff and there was a lot of blood! The bottoms of the casts were completely soaked in blood. I became instantly terrified. I screamed out loud and started crying hysterically. The last thing I remember before passing out was a nurse running toward my bed.

The next thing I remember is my family coming to visit. My brother and sister were with my parents. Shortly after coming into my room, my brother started to cry when he saw the blood soaked casts and asked what they had done to me. My dad was quick to criticize him for crying too and told him to leave the room so I wouldn't get upset again.

The conversation going on inside my anesthetically and intoxicated head was something like:

1. What did they do to me? Why is there so much blood? Didn't they sew me back up? Why am I so groggy? What is going on!?!
2. Wow. My big brother got in trouble for crying too! Crying is *really* bad.

The conclusions I arrived at were:

1. Hospitals are scary places – referenced, reinforced, validated, and a colored filter added to represent the intensity of the fear.
2. What did they do to me? Although this is a question, it is still a conclusion, and one that would be referenced many times to come. This conclusion is filed in my FEAR cabinet.

3. Crying is bad and it doesn't matter who cries, you'll get in trouble. Although there is a variation on the original conclusion, the idea that crying is bad is still referenced, reinforced, and validated. Another colored filter is added to the file and it is refiled in the FEAR cabinet.

The next morning, the surgeon brought medical students to my room. I remember them discussing my case as if I wasn't even there! As a kid, I didn't understand the idea of a teaching hospital; it just felt like everyone was staring and judging me.

A few days' post-op, I was loaded into an ambulance and taken to the Shriner`s Hospital which sat alongside the Red River in Winnipeg. It was a beautiful location. I remember a large patio area that overlooked the river. There were tall trees along the banks of the river and on the hospital grounds. I immediately felt safe there.

This time, I was released after only a few days later and my mom and I flew back to Regina. My dad had taken my brother and sister back with him the day after my surgery. I was to return in a couple of weeks to get the stitches out, take x-rays to make sure everything is good, and re-cast for the remaining month.

Two weeks later, we were back in Winnipeg to get my stitches out, have more x-rays to ensure that everything was healing properly and re-cast. I remember being nervous about how exactly they were going to get the casts off. As soon as the cast saw started, I became extremely scared. I tried to get off the table and away from the saw. I was wailing. Tears were flowing from my eyes like a waterfall. The orderly whose job was to get the cast off was trying to calm me down, explaining that the saw wouldn't hurt *me* – only the cast. He was quite patient, but my dad was getting more and more agitated the louder I wailed. He started yelling at me to settle down and keep still. He held me down on the table and told me to "Quit being such a baby." The orderly was then able to cut both casts off. I could see that the skin on my legs was very dry and caked with blood.

Once the casts were off, I thought I was over the worst part and I started to calm down. Now, however, it was time to take out the stitches. There was dried blood from the incisions and a fine layer of skin had already grown over top of the stiches, which made the task of taking them out all the more painful.

The conversation going on inside my head was something like:

1. I don't like coming to this place. They hurt me every time and I get scared and then I cry, and then I get in trouble. This is a bad place.

The conclusion I arrived at was

1. Hospitals are scary – once again referenced, reinforced, validated, and a colored filter added to represent the intensity of the fear. The file is re-filed in the FEAR cabinet.
2. Crying is/ I am bad – once again referenced, reinforced, validated, and a colored filter added to represent the intensity of the fear. The file is re-filed in the FEAR cabinet.

Finally, it was all over, and the new casts were on. X-rays had confirmed everything was on track, and we headed back to Regina. I would return to get the casts off for good and for physical rehabilitation.

Mom and I flew to Winnipeg together four weeks later. We arrived at the Children's Hospital and checked in. The casts were taken off, and new x-rays taken. There were new and different tests done on my legs. My mom stayed with me in Winnipeg until all the tests were done, and I was transferred to the Shriner's Hospital were we were shown to the room in which I would spend the next several weeks. My mom couldn't stay with me because she had to help my dad work in the store.

There were lots of other kids here with lots of different kinds of injuries. Two of the kids had been in a bad house fire. I still remember those two kids as if it were yesterday. The fire had badly burned the skin on their entire bodies, taken their eyelids, ears, and most of their fingers. Their skin was so thin you could almost see through it. They wore a protective body sock that looked kind of like a wetsuit. I remember asking the nurse one day why no one came to visit them, and she explained as gently as she could that their parents had given them up to the courts because of the way they looked due to their burns. I was horrified. Their parents gave them away because they had been burned and because they were DIFFERENT?!

The conversation going on in my mind went something like:

1. If I am different, and they are different, and they were given away because they were different, then I could be too!

The conclusion I arrived at was:

1. If you are damaged, no one wants you – this conclusion is filed in my FEAR cabinet.

I've always had a curiosity about things and was eager to learn what the nurse was doing, and I missed my mom. I became the nurse's biggest little helper! Because I was eager to learn and be helpful, she taught me how to take respiration, blood pressure readings, and pulse rate, and had me record the numbers on a chart that had all of our names on it. I felt so grown up. I decided right then and there that I would be a nurse when I finally did grow up.

One day, a physiotherapist took me into the stairwell to practice going up and down the stairs. I moved toward the railing, so I could hang on to it. I had always gone up and down stairs hanging on to a railing. The therapist asked me why I moved towards the railing, and I told her I would fall if I didn't hang on. She told me it was all in my head, and she insisted I go up and down the stairs without holding on. I was really scared of falling. If I fell, I would have to stay here and maybe even have to get cut open again, but I didn't want to get into trouble. I was afraid that if they told my dad I misbehaved, I would really get into trouble when I got home.

After a few weeks I was allowed to go home. Because I was so young, a nurse from the hospital had to take me to the airport and put me in the custody of the airline attendants. I was excited to fly by myself and felt very grown up. The flight from Winnipeg to Regina is only an hour, and that hour goes fast when you are fascinated by everything going on around you. When we landed, I had to wait for the other passengers to exit the plane before the attendant would walk me to baggage claim where my parents were waiting for me. My mom was so excited to see me! She was crying, and we ran towards each other and embraced. I was so happy to be home! My dad looked at me sadly and said out loud, "You still walk with a limp! Why are you still limping?" I was devastated. I felt a lump rise up in my throat, but I didn't cry. I hung my head in shame. I don't remember anything after that.

I can't even describe how worthless I felt in that moment. All I could think of was those two burned kids and how their parents had given them away because they were different and were never going to be 'normal.' I still limped all right, and it was only going to get worse.

As it would turn out, this foot surgery did nothing to improve my gait, keep me from falling down all the time, or alleviate any pain. This early experience created a negative picture about doctors, nurses, physiotherapists, surgeries, and hospitals in general. Every time my feelings were hurt while I was in hospital, regardless of the specific situation, the perception that hospital experiences resulted in pain was reinforced, as well as the conclusion that I wasn't good enough because of the 'problem with my hips.'

CHAPTER 13

RECALLING AND HEALING A PAINFUL MEMORY

~With God, all things are possible.~

Some memories get buried very deep in the back of the filing cabinets of your mind because the emotions tied to the more especially traumatic experiences are too intense to be used as references. Additionally, there isn't usually a conclusion for these experiences. Instead there is confusion about how an experience of that nature could have even taken place.

The memory of having been raped at 13 didn't even find its way into my conscious thought until I was in my forties. To this day, I can still only recall some of the details, and the only conclusion I ever had was a question: why did he do this to me? Despite not having an answer I now know that this man might have used my body for his pleasure, but the essence of who I am was never touched.

Sometimes, during especially difficult or traumatic experiences, a person only feels shock, and feelings of sadness and fear that should have been present are absent. The shock quickly turns into anger, and the conclusion becomes one of justification – if he/she hadn't done such and such, I wouldn't be behaving this way. Every time your mind uses this type of file as a reference, the justification is reinforced, it becomes a resentment, and you are that victim over and over again in your mind. When you refuse to allow yourself to feel the sadness, grief, anger, rage, or whichever emotions are being denied, you are only prolonging your suffering, and eventually these denied feelings will manifest physically. High blood pressure, angina and other coronary problems, diabetes, chronic fatigue syndrome, fibromy-algia, and chronic depression are just some of the diseases that find their way into the physical body after trauma.

It is important to understand that to heal from traumatic experiences, you need to allow yourself to feel all the feelings that present themselves. In doing this, it not only allows you to reassess the initial file, it also releases the anger, resentment, and bitterness from your body. Especially traumatic experiences should be reviewed and reassessed with a qualified professional of your choosing. Working with a qualified counselor can help you under-stand the experience from a different perspective and to integrate it.

EVERY UNHEALED EXPERIENCE IS ANOTHER BRICK IN YOUR WALL

No one likes to have their feelings hurt. No one likes to feel sad all the time. No one wants to be angry or resentful or bitter either, but there are a lot of folks who are. Most of the time, they just don't know how to get rid of all the negative feelings floating around inside their minds. They don't know that every single file in their FEAR cabinet causes them to create a barrier around the place in their being where they feel.

Every negative experience is just another brick in your protective wall, and before a person can truly feel pure and unconditional love, that wall is going to need to come down. One by one, each brick that is a resentment, which is nothing more than a negative memory, which is nothing more than a file with a negative conclusion, must be consciously reviewed and reassessed at your current level of understanding.

Remember, when the initial file was created you were only a child, and that child is the one hanging on to the file with both hands, both legs, and both feet. The child within you is the part of your mind that thinks about what happened and creates stories. That child is the part of you that is still scared, lonely, angry and resentful. That child needs to know and feel that it was never alone, and that a lot of the things that he/she experienced might not have happened quite the way they thought.

SELF WORTH & SELF LOVE

The root of a person's misery really boils down to a lack of self worth, and when the files in a person's FEAR cabinet outnumber the files in their LOVE cabinet, true self-worth is impossible. You might think that you value yourself, but if there are conditions attached to that value – a degree, a title, a certain weight, a certain look – then you value the attachment and not yourself. If there is defiance behind your claims of self worth – that is, if you feel a need to defend yourself – then you think you value yourself, but you don't *know* you do. If you feel the need to point out someone else's flaws, or chastise them for their beliefs, you do not know your own worth.

There is no defiance in love and loving yourself unconditionally is the beginning of knowing your worth. Loving one's self has nothing to do with the image you see in the mirror. It means that you don't see your size or shape, your intelligence level, your accomplishments, or the amount of money in your bank account. It has nothing to do with who you have sex with, how you dress, what your hair style is, or who you know. Loving yourself unconditionally means there are no labels attached to who you are, because labels are conditions. If you associate yourself with a label, there are files in your FEAR cabinet telling you that you *are* that label and that you must defend that label at all costs. Those files are getting in the way of your peace.

Labels are for things, not people. Labels are descriptions, not human beings. Labels have become so important to people today, that there is now more division among human beings than ever before. Every group of people that identify themselves with a label stands in defiance of every other group, but the irony is there would be no reason to find a group that one fits in if people didn't feel the need to have labels and to defend that label. Acceptance, like everything else, begins with yourself. You can't give away what you don't possess, and that means that you will not be able to accept others until you've accepted yourself. Once you accept yourself, the need for the label disappears.

Problems in our lives arise when our initial perception has created a solid perspective that is consistently used as a reference point. The word problem is defined as something that is difficult to deal with or solve, so although problems might seem difficult, they are just puzzles that have a solution.

You might have even convinced yourself that you have grown past your emotionally painful experiences and left them behind, so that when you are experiencing a similar negative experience, you can't understand why it's happening all over again and become frustrated. The thing is, similar unpleasant experiences will continue to happen until you actually deal with the initial file, reassess the conclusion, heal it, or render it invalid and irrelevant to your current state of being.

CHAPTER 14

DIET, NUTRITIONAL DEFICIENCIES, AND YOUR OVERALL HEALTH

The body is a complex structure containing trillions of microscopic life forms. Each microscopic life form communicates and cooperates with all the other microscopic life forms inside your body, and it is this communication and cooperation that keeps our hearts beating, our stomachs digesting, our bodies walking, talking, breathing, and thinking. Every molecule has a job to do, and they require the right fuel to perform their job. We fuel our bodies with water and with food. If we don't give our bodies adequate nutrients, then it will become imbalanced and will malfunction.

Nutrients are more than just vitamins, and the quality of the nutrients we take in is just as important as the quantity. The cleaner the fuel, the more efficient the body will run. Nutrients include water, amino acids or proteins, beneficial bacteria, carbohydrates, fats, as well as water and fat-soluble vitamins and minerals. The specific amount of each nutrient that your body requires is as unique to you as your fingerprint.

The state of health of your body is in is always up to you. Not a doctor – not the health department or the government – you! You choose the lifestyle you live, and that lifestyle greatly affects your physical health. Your thoughts drive your body, not the other way around. Your perceptions about you, your body and its importance will determine the quality and quantity of attention you choose to give to it. If you believe you are worth the effort, then the foods you choose will be from the cleanest source possible. If you find and recognize that your body is in a state of nutritional depletion that food alone will not resolve, you will be willing to invest in supplements to ensure your body's nutritional demands are adequately met.

Every person has unique nutritional requirements that are dependent on several different factors that include: typical diet, current level of health, intensity and amount of exercise, use of prescription medications for a diagnosed illness that use nutrients as co-factors to properly assimilate in the body, patterns of recreational behavior, and acute injury caused by a fall or car accident, among others.

If your days are hectic, you are more likely to choose pre-packaged foods or eat out more often. Cooking meals from scratch takes time, and if you don't have the time or the right foods on hand, it's easier to just microwave something that was commercially prepared. The problem is, processed foods generally have higher amounts of sugar, contain preservatives and other chemicals that may strip your body of nutrients, or cause adverse reactions.

If you have had several bouts of cold or flu, your immune system weakens which can create additional demands for specific nutrients such as vitamins A, C and the mineral zinc. If you were prescribed antibiotics for your illness, your intestinal system will need to be replenished with good bacteria, so a probiotic supplement should be considered. Chronic illnesses such as celiac disease adversely affect nutrient absorption, and some medications taken for acid reflux can negatively impact and change the way your body digests foods.

If you have been diagnosed with or have a higher risk factor for heart disease, you may benefit from extra B vitamins, vitamin C, essential fatty acids, CoQ10 and garlic. Certain medications may interact with supplements or herbal remedies, so you should always check with a qualified health practitioner before adding a new supplement.

If you participate in a regular exercise routine such as high impact cardio training or heavy weight lifting, you may require extra protein and extra minerals such as calcium, magnesium, and potassium. Gentle exercise routines such as Tai Chi or some forms of yoga will help to keep your muscles limber, while some competitive sports may create tight or strained muscles. Muscles require specific nutrients like protein and magnesium (as well as others) to maintain their strength. Not exercising at all means your body cannot effectively get rid of all the toxic and unnecessary substances it temporarily stores in your lymphatic system.

Stress, accidents and surgeries can also create additional demands on your nutritional requirements. Digestion is slowed down and sometimes halted depending on the level of stress your mind believes it is experiencing. The type of stress your body is feeling doesn't matter as far as your adrenal system is concerned – the toll on these glands and other parts of your body will be the same regardless.

The state of your emotional health directly affects how your body will call for and utilize nutrients. Untreated anxiety, trauma-related disorders, grief, and even anger will eventually take a toll on your physical health. A high-stress lifestyle – both personal and work related – can be especially draining if you don't have adequate emotional support and will also deplete your body's stores of certain vitamins and minerals needed to maintain good health.

We are three dimensional beings: body, mind, and spirit. Each part is connected to the other, so when one is out of balance, the others will follow.

CHAPTER 15

PERSONAL POWER RETURNS

*~ Corrective learning always begins with the awakening of Spirit,
and the turning away from the belief in physical sight.*
~ Helen Schucman, A Course in Miracles

When you have made the commitment to yourself to change, you invite Grace into your life. Once most of the files in your FEAR cabinet have been reviewed and healed, you will feel lighter. The weight of the resentments and anger that you were carrying leaves your body, and the protective wall you've built around your heart falls one brick at a time. When those bricks fall, light can find a way in. Where there is light, there is also warmth. Your mind can learn how to be understanding and compassionate towards others. Most of all – you open yourself to receive God's truth and experience peace and joy.

As your FEAR cabinet empties, you can now look to your LOVE cabinet to remind yourself of all the things you did and all the things that you had that you can now allow yourself to be grateful for. Your LOVE cabinet is filled with conclusions you arrived at in times where you felt free, happy, and loved. The experience of buying and wearing your favorite jeans is in a file in that cabinet. Your favorite sweater, T-shirt, and your favorite scent of bubble-bath! The best kind of ice cream to eat is in a file in that cabinet somewhere, and all the people that were kind to you are described in a file in your LOVE cabinet. Your favorite thing to do outside in the heat of the summer sun is in a file in that cabinet, and a description of all the snow angels you made is in a file in the LOVE cabinet.

Your accomplishments are in your LOVE cabinet! All the tests you passed in school are in a file in your LOVE cabinet. Learning to ride a bike, swim, dance, and skate on ice is in a file in your LOVE cabinet. Having the skills required and being accepted for your first job is in your LOVE cabinet, and every promotion you were eligible for is in your LOVE cabinet. Baking your first cake, building your first snowman, and changing a flat tire is in a file in your LOVE cabinet. Graduating school and receiving a diploma is described in a file in your LOVE cabinet and going to the after-grad party and celebrating with all of your friends in is a file in your LOVE cabinet.

You might think as you read this right now, that you don't have a single solitary file in your LOVE cabinet, but I assure you, you do! Reminding yourself of all the things you had and did in your life that were good helps your mind to start to assess what is going on around it now in a positive light. Start a new section in your journal, and as you remember them, write down all the things that made you proud of yourself!

RETRAINING YOUR MIND IN A NEW PROCESS

Your mind is not going to let go of the habit of heading to the FEAR cabinet first, because it's done that for many years, but your mind is not the boss of you – you are!

When your mind doesn't have the files from the FEAR cabinet it always used to reference certain things, it will dig deep in the cabinets to find one. The thing about those files is, the emotions attached to them are far less intense, so you will be able to consciously and mindfully tell your mind to put that file back where it found it and assess your current situation without using a past file at all. If your mind does manage to find a file that has some intense emotions attached, it just means you missed that one the first go around. Reassess that file and put it away for good!

Every minute of every day is a new experience, and I am certain that when you add up the minutes that you feel free and content in a day, you will find that they far outnumber the minutes that you felt unsure and confused.

STAGES OF LEARNING

Learning to assess what is going on around you at your current level of understanding, without using any past reference is going to take some time, and a lot of practice. We learn in stages, and the best description of these learning stages that I've seen is described in *Thorsons Way of NLP* by Joseph O'Connor and Ian McDermott.

In NLP (Neuro-Linguistic Programming) there are four stages of learning:

a. Unconscious incompetence – You've never tried; you don't know how to do something & you don't know that you don't know how to do something.

b. Conscious incompetence – you start doing things differently. You know enough to know you aren't good at it, and it takes a lot of your conscious attention. This stage of learning is uncomfortable, but it is in this stage where you learn the most.

c. Conscious competence – You can do it, you have reached the capability level, but it still takes a lot of your attention.

d. Unconscious competence – You do it easily without thinking.

DON'T BE AFRAID TO FACE OBSTACLES

There will always be obstacles or hurdles to get over. Life is full of challenges, but by now, I hope you are beginning to understand that you are always in control of your own life.

When you have made the decision to change your life for the better, there will be some family members and friends that aren't willing or ready to go down the new path with you. As you regain your inner strength and the true essence of who you really are gains strength, people challenge that strength. Learning to stand your ground without attacking or criticizing the people around you is just part of the process of retraining your mind to see and assess your current situation at your current level of understanding.

By cleaning out your own FEAR cabinet and forgiving yourself as well as all the people you thought hurt you, you will understand that everyone is just like you were, doing the best they can. Remind yourself when people challenge you, that they too, are viewing life through the files contained in their own FEAR cabinet.

HEALING MEANS FEELING

Allowing yourself to feel whatever it is you are feeling in the moment, without lashing out at others is all part of the process. No one lives a life without negative feelings. Pain, sorrow, grief, sadness, and anger are just parts of what it means to be human. If you didn't feel anger, you would never know joy. If you hadn't experienced grief and loss, you wouldn't be able to recognize what appreciation and gratitude feel like.

Here are some questions to ask yourself every time you find yourself out of balance.

1. What is at the root of my malcontent? Why am I not happy?
2. What expectation did I have that isn't being met?
3. Where did that expectation come from? What did I think I was going to gain?
4. What will happen to me if that expectation is never met? What am I going to lose?
5. Am I willing to forgive the person who did not meet or live up to my expectation?
6. Am I ready to learn the truth of the expectation and forgive the person who did not meet or live up to my expectation?
7. After learning the truth, do I completely understand and feel compassion toward the person who did not live up to my expectation?
8. Have I completely let go of the expectation, and have I completely resolved all the feelings associated with the expectation?
9. Have I hurt anyone in the process of working through this expectation? If so, have I apologized and done my best to make amends?
10. Have I forgiven myself for having the expectation in the first place, and I am truly ready to move on?

Get in the habit of looking inward whenever you find yourself feeling as if things are not going the way you thought they should. Every time you go through this process, it gets a little easier and resolves itself a little faster. Don't give up on yourself!

You are a child of God and that alone makes you matter. You are the creator of your own life, and you have been given everything that you need to become who you were meant to be. Find the gifts within that you have been given and use them. You can accomplish anything you set your mind to!

CPSIA information can be obtained
at www.ICGtesting.com
Printed in the USA
LVHW07s1001310518
578692LV00002B/1/P

9 781525 524110